D0649616

Educational Planning and Expenditure Decisions in Developing Countries

Robert W. McMeekin, Jr.

The Praeger Special Studies program—utilizing the most modern and efficient book production techniques and a selective worldwide distribution network—makes available to the academic, government, and business communities significant, timely research in U.S. and international economic, social, and political development.

Educational Planning and Expenditure Decisions in Developing Countries

With a Malaysian Case Study

PRAEGER SPECIAL STUDIES IN INTERNATIONAL ECONOMICS AND DEVELOPMENT

Praeger Publishers New York Washington London

Library of Congress Cataloging in Publication Data

McMeekin, Robert W
    Education planning and expenditure decisions in
developing countries : with a Malaysian case study.

    (Praeger special studies in international economics
and development)
    Bibliography: p.
    Includes index.
    1. Educational planning—Malaysia.   2. Education—
Economic aspects—Malaysia. I. Title.
LA1236.M24   338.4'3   74-9411
ISBN 0-275-09590-8

Library
I.U.P.
Indiana, Pa.

379.5951 M 227 e
C. 1

PRAEGER PUBLISHERS
111 Fourth Avenue, New York, N.Y. 10003, U.S.A.
5, Cromwell Place, London SW7 2JL, England

Published in the United States of America in 1975
by Praeger Publishers, Inc.

All rights reserved

© 1975 by Praeger Publishers, Inc.

Printed in the United States of America

For Diana

ACKNOWLEDGMENTS

Preparation of this study was made possible by a Travel and Study Grant from the Ford Foundation, 1972-1973. Dr. Reuben Frodin, who supervised the grant, has provided suggestions and encouragement throughout the course of the work. Earlier versions of portions of Chapters 1, 2, and 3 were prepared in connection with a study entitled <u>Financing and Efficiency in Education,</u> conducted by Harvard's Center for Studies of Education and Development (CSED) for the U.S. Agency for International Development. I am indebted to Professor Manuel Zymelman, the author of that study, for comments on the earlier papers and permission to use the material here. The views expressed are my own, however, and do not represent an official position of the Ford Foundation or any other institution, agency or individual.

During a visiting professorship at Harvard (1967-1968), Professor Roland McKean set forth his views on economic analysis as a "way of looking at problems" of public expenditure choice, which have provided an intellectual framework for much of the present work. My own dissatisfaction with the most frequently used approaches to educational planning—especially the quantitative projections, manpower, and rate of return approaches, as usually applied—grew out of five years' experience as planning advisor to the Ministries of Education of El Salvador, Nicaragua and, most recently, Malaysia. My appreciation to many colleagues in these ministries and various international education agencies for their cooperation, insights, and friendship cannot be adequately expressed here. I am especially grateful to the directors of Malaysia's Education Planning and Research Division, Murad bin Mohammed Noor and his predecessor S. V. J. Ponniah, who provided the "go ahead" for much of the research that underlies the case studies of Chapters 4 and 5.

Particular gratitude is due to two individuals. Harold S. Beebout, who conducted the secondary school sample survey discussed in Chapter 4 and Appendix B, and I. Lourdesamy, who performed the longitudinal survey of vocational school graduates treated in Chapter 5, shared many of their ideas during the conduct of these studies and generously made their data available to me. Members of the staff of Malaysia's Examinations Syndicate programmed the flow model of the Malaysian education system outlined in Appendix C. Ms. Helene Tuchman prepared the index.

Professors Arthur Smithies and Dwight Perkins of Harvard have made constructive criticisms that greatly strengthened the study.

Professors Mark Blaug and C. Arnold Anderson made comments on earlier papers incorporated in the present work. Despite help and insights from many quarters, responsibility for errors of fact or interpretation is entirely my own.

LIST OF TABLES

LIST OF FIGURES

Educational Planning and Expenditure Decisions in Developing Countries

This study addresses a set of interrelated problems concerning the management and planning of developing education systems. These problems include: (1) shortcomings of the best-known approaches to educational planning as usually applied, (2) the orientation of most planning efforts toward high-level allocative decisions, and (3) the limitations of data available for policy analysis. Most countries of the world carry on some form of planning for the development of their education systems. In many cases these planning efforts are little more than attempts to project recent trends in enrollment growth into the future, calculate the number of teachers and classroom places needed to accommodate this growth, and estimate the budgetary requirements for providing the needed facilities and teachers.

Such quantitative and nonanalytical planning developed during periods when enrollments in most developing countries were extremely low. In that circumstance the mere provision of more education was the dominant problem and unsophisticated planning was at least partially satisfactory. Many early education plans suffered from problems of internal inconsistency, infeasibility of targets and, hence, nonimplementation. In the context of large unmet demand for access to education, however, the disadvantages of merely projecting growth into the future were not particularly great.

In recent years increasing numbers of developing countries have achieved more nearly satisfactory enrollment ratios, often approaching 90 percent of the school age population at the primary level. With rapid increases in enrollment, education budgets have also increased. Education's budgetary demands absorb up to 25 or even 30 percent of all public expenditures in many developing countries, and other claims on public resources now compete strongly with education. The need for more sophisticated planning approaches is far greater under these conditions and planners have sought better ways of determining how much to spend on education and on what projects. Two approaches to educational planning have been dominant. One has involved attempts to measure the economy's manpower needs and to adjust the education system so as to provide the right balance of graduates. Another approach, advanced by economists, has been to calculate the economic returns to different sorts and levels of education and allocate resources to those forms of education that yield the highest returns. The usual applications of these approaches have had serious shortcomings. The purpose of this book is to suggest a change in the orientation of educational planning.

Efforts to achieve orderly and efficient development of education systems through planning have not been notably successful for a variety of reasons. Education systems consist of complex, many layered, interrelated groups of activities that are even difficult to describe and comprehend. The analytical approaches to planning—even the most sophisticated applications of manpower and rate-of-return planning—do not provide adequate guidance for policy choices; especially when the choices involve multiple objectives, intangible results and nonlinear relationships. The information needed to conduct systematic analysis and planning is seriously limited (although vast quantities of relatively useless data exist). And education systems have particular characteristics, especially difficulties of measuring inputs and outputs, that make analysis and planning more difficult than in most other sectors.

A considerable literature has developed on the subject of educational planning, in which various methodological approaches have been advanced. Controversy between the manpower and the rate-of-return approaches to shaping educational policy has filled a substantial portion of this literature. Linear programming (based upon either manpower or rate-of-return premises) has been proposed as a methodological tool and a branch of the literature has addressed different ways to apply maximizing techniques. Much of the argument has been carried on by economists concerned with education. Despite the attention devoted to the subject, a gulf exists between the subject matter treated in the literature and the problems confronted by working planners at the sectoral level. In part this has been due to the tendency of "discipline-oriented" economists to address questions of macro-allocation while their "problem-oriented" colleagues in ministry planning offices are concerned with micro-allocation questions.[1] There has also been a strong tendency for theoreticians to seek single approaches leading to optimal solutions.

Given the difficulties of planning educational systems, it is not realistic to expect economic analysis to produce "right" or optimal solutions to complex policy problems. It is possible, however, to use economic analysis and related tools to provide information that

2

will guide decision makers in changing education systems for the better. It is possible to make education systems somewhat more efficient in performing their functions. Better information for policy analysis can certainly be produced. Analytical methods can be modified and applied to the problems faced by planners and administrators in the real world. This study attempts to make a contribution to these ends.

DEFINITION OF EDUCATIONAL PLANNING

Before considering some of the best-known approaches to educational planning, it would be well to define the process for purposes of this discussion. As understood in this study, educational planning is the continuous process of providing information to decision makers on how well the education system is accomplishing its goals and how the cost-effectiveness of such accomplishment can be improved. This attempt at definition differs from most of the best-known definitions of educational planning, some of which will be discussed below. Let us examine it in more detail.

Educational planning here refers to sectoral programming as distinct from the central planner's task of attempting to determine the education sector's share of total fiscal resources. The latter question is important but it differs fundamentally from the question of what to do with the sector's share once it has been determined. There is, of course, a close relationship between how much is spent on education and what it is spent on. The discussion that follows, however, is principally concerned with the latter question. To cite an example, planning as defined here is concerned not with whether to invest in, say, primary vs. secondary education (as macro-level analyses typically are) but rather with such questions as: how much to spend on vocational as opposed to general secondary education; how specific vocational training should be; what trade specialties are most readily accepted in the labor market; what balance between classroom time and workshop time equips graduates best for the world of work, and so on. These questions of internal allocation are the subject of sectoral planning and programming.

Planning is a continuous process in the definition above. It is not merely a periodic, convulsive effort to establish investment targets for five or more years. Such exercises are characteristic of many central planning efforts. At the sectoral level, however, the major questions faced by decision makers recur, change, and develop within much shorter periods. Typically the decisions involve both capital and recurrent expenditures (the relationship between the two becomes increasingly intimate at lower levels of decision), and choices must

3

be made annually or even more frequently. The planner's role is one of illuminating, as much as is possible, these frequent intra-sectoral choices.

There are a number of convergent bodies of thought that view social organizations and institutions as cybernetic mechanisms: that is as goal-oriented systems that are controlled and directed on the basis of "feedback." Richard Stone calls attention to various ways in which economic thought has viewed economies as self-regulating systems, with particular problems of communication and control, since long before Wiener proposed the term cybernetics.[2] Other writers have explored the cybernetic nature of organizations and the role of information in guiding their development.[3] While it is recognized that education systems do not truly fit the definition of "open systems" and that they are far from self-regulating mechanisms, educational planning does serve as an element in a "feedback loop" that influences the course of development of the system. It is this view of educational planning as part of a cybernetic process that underlies the definition given above, especially the role of planning as providing a flow of information to decision makers. Education systems are public services subject to the decision and control of administrators who (nominally) seek to accomplish public goals. Such systems lack the automatic, self-regulating characteristics of open economies, which tend toward efficient resource allocation. If education systems fail to regulate themselves efficiently, the position of this study is that this is due in considerable part to failure in the supply and use of information.

It is something of a commonplace to remark upon the need for liaison between planning and administration of education programs.[4] If there is no such liaison, planning as defined here is failing totally in its task. The purpose of planning is to improve the quality of the choices made by the responsible decision makers by giving them better information and analyses upon which to base their decisions. If the information does not find its way into the decision making process, then the feedback loop is not closed and the purpose of planning is defeated. If planning is truly understood as a tool of management, then a disjunction between planning and administration is unlikely to occur. Some writers see other roles for planning, as will be discussed below,[5] but the role addressed in this discussion is one of information for administrative decisions.

The information generated and transmitted concerns the degree to which the education system is accomplishing its goals. The concept of educational goals is fraught with intrinsic difficulty and affected by considerable controversy. Some writers object that you cannot set goals for an educational project or program.[6] Others hold that, whether or not goals can be set, there are times when they should not be.[7] It is a conviction underlying the present definition of planning that, within limits, it is possible and desirable to clarify the aims of educational programs. If planners and policy makers succeed in clarifying goals and providing information on how well programs are achieving them, then economic analysis of expenditure choices can aid in the efficient achievement of those goals.

What do we mean by "efficient achievement" in education? This brings us to the last element in the definition: cost-effectiveness as the criterion of choice. Cost-effectiveness is a central element in the conceptual framework for analysis of education programs discussed in this study. Briefly, cost-effectiveness can be explained as getting the most for your money: either obtaining the maximum return in terms of your objectives for a fixed budget, or alternatively, obtaining a given level of objectives at the lowest cost. The concept seems simple but it is apparently not intuitively obvious, as C. J. Hitch has observed.[8] Once grasped, however, the concept of cost-effectiveness is a powerful analytical tool.

It will be noted that the future-oriented nature of planning is not stressed. The definition differs intentionally in this respect from most of the classic definitions of planning. Planning does indeed involve charting a course of action for the future and establishing a strategy for goal accomplishment. The basis for such forward planning, however, lies in the operation of the existing education system in the present and recent past. Education systems are not planned from some zero-state. Any planning effort is directed toward modification of an existing system—often a large, old, well-entrenched, traditional and intractable system. "Planning" then becomes a matter of designing strategies for change in the present system. It looks to the future, but it does so in terms of ways in which the existing system can be incrementally modified in order to accomplish its complex set of objectives somewhat more satisfactorily than at present. Planning viewed in this light becomes, importantly, a process of evaluating the existing education system at the level of its component programs and subprograms.

Any consideration of the definition of educational planning would be incomplete without reference to the important essay by C. A. Anderson and M. J. Bowman, "Theoretical Considerations in Educational Planning."[9] The authors take as their point of departure Dror's definition of planning: "The process of preparing a set of decisions for action in the future, directed at achieving goals by optimal means."[10] Analyzing this definition a phrase at a time, the authors develop their own definition adapted to the planning of education systems.

Anderson and Bowman accept the concept of "preparing a set of decisions for action," noting a need for a theoretical distinction

5

between planning, implementation, and decision making in order to avoid "endless disputes" on the scope of planning.[11] This theoretical distinction is in some conflict with the definition of planning offered here, but the difference is not central to the main thesis. Anderson and Bowman note later that "a continuous planning process with operational relevance will entail continuous feed-backs of experience, including experience in the implementation (or non-implementation) of prior plans or phases of plans."[12] Thus their view foreshadows the one presented here with respect to the relationship between past, present, and future in planning and the relationship between planning and administration; even to the use of the feedback concept.

A major difference between Dror's definition and the one developed by Anderson and Bowman lies in the phrase: "directed at achieving goals by optimal means." The authors take exception to the concept of optimality, stating that: "To strive for optimization would be a negation of operationally effective planning as an action-oriented process in a dynamic world."[13] In rejecting optimality the authors also omit the rest of the phrase, "directed at achieving goals," with no further comment. This is an important omission and one that conflicts directly with the definition of planning offered here. While optimality is an unsatisfactory criterion for the "set of decisions" that planners prepare, the truncated definition that the authors retain offers no criterion for decision at all; not even the concept of "satisficing" that they mention elsewhere.[14] If Dror's phrase were modified to read, "directed at achieving goals by cost-effective means," there would be no major conflict between that definition and the one offered here. The remainder of the Anderson and Bowman essay presents a valuable review of the field of educational planning, including the manpower approach, Tinbergen's fixed-coefficient models, and rate-of-return analysis.

Another outlook on educational planning is found in Kjell Eide's essay, "Organization of Education Planning."[15] Eide approaches education planning in terms of its organizational effect, which gives a slightly different perspective on the subject. Throughout the paper he emphasizes (correctly) the political nature of the planning-cum-administrative function. The ideal role of the planner is seen to be "increasing the degree of rationality in the political decision making, through exploring the possibilities for basing such decisions on empirical evidence. . . ."[16] This view is fully consonant with the definitions discussed above. It differs in that it sees planning not only as a process leading to change in education programs, but also as an agent for change in the administration of the programs and associated decision making.

Eide sees planning as a gadfly activity, often at odds with the administrative hierarchy. It is a vector of innovation and change that, because it would alter the existing order, tends toward conflict with proponents of the present scheme of things. This view reveals an important dimension of planning not apparent from the definition proposed here. As will be discussed further in the following chapters, planning involves choices between an array of alternatives, including new ways of performing educational activities. The role of planning set forth earlier—providing information for decision makers—may produce information that is disturbing or critical of existing practices. If the gadfly role becomes too abrasive, however, the linkage of credibility and confidence between planner and administrator is damaged; and with it the role of planning as an element in the continuing feedback loop.

Many other attempts at definition can be found in the literature. Beeby feels that this is inevitable in view of the amorphous state of the family of activities related to planning educational development.[17] Variations between alternative definitions do not mean, according to Beeby, that some are necessarily wrong; but rather that their authors have different perspectives and emphasize different aspects of the process. The present discussion makes no pretense to completeness. It proposes only to present one more definition, for use in this study, and to consider a few other comments that add dimensions to the definition offered here.

MAJOR APPROACHES TO EDUCATIONAL PLANNING

This section reviews the major approaches to educational planning in terms of their principal strengths and weaknesses. The literature concerning these approaches is very extensive and this work cannot presume to review each definitively. The brief explanations probably do the approaches an injustice by omitting many subtle points, but selected references cited provide a much fuller understanding of the approaches.[18]

Quantitative Projections

Studies of educational planning have rarely dignified with a name the exercises in applied arithmetic that are carried out in probably the majority of the Ministries of Education throughout the world in the name of educational planning. This "approach" consists mainly in projecting the growth of the existing system, largely by extrapolating recent trends five or perhaps ten years into the future. Some attempts have been made to refine the methods of projection and to urge that questions about efficiency, cost, and possible alternative programs be asked in conjunction with the projection exercises.[19]

But there is no foundation for analysis and choice in such planning; it merely projects more of the existing forms of education. One should perhaps not be too hasty in condemning this approach. It does not involve analysis of alternatives. It does not make use of economic science to inform investment choices. It is, however, closely related to the problems and aims of the sector and its many practitioners often take into account the nature, content, and the complex articulation of the subsector activities that constitute the sector program. This cannot be said of all approaches.

Much of the technical assistance provided to education planning in the nineteen sixties aimed at improving the basic data and methodologies for quantitative projections. Given that many countries lacked basic data on enrollment, wastage, teacher supplies, and so on, these efforts were not without benefits. Such data and projections, while a necessary condition for planning, are far from a sufficient condition. One obvious shortcoming is that some strategy for educational development was needed, as opposed to simply projecting increases in the existing system. Early attempts to provide a strategy were often based upon some assessment of "national needs" or "social demand."

Social Demand

A modification of the quantitative projection approach is found where countries have adopted major targets, often on the basis of political desirability or for international prestige and compliance with regional "norms," without analysis of these targets to determine whether they are economically or culturally desirable (or, for that matter, even feasible). Such targets as "universal primary education" by a given date, or some arbitrary proportion of secondary enrollment in vocational schools by a certain time are handed down from above. They may be based on popular pressure for more school places or on someone's estimate that achieving the target would be beneficial. The task of the planner is to determine what rates of growth in enrollment, pupil places available, teachers, and other inputs would be necessary to meet the "requirement" or "demand."[20] Again no optimizing or suboptimizing technique is applied. The existing education system is simply expanded in much the same form until the target is reached (or perhaps a shift in main ingredients is made, with the ingredients remaining the same). The so-called international comparisons approach is a modification of the same sort of planning.[21] Here the targets are derived from other countries' histories at times that are assumed to be analogous to the stage of development desired at the end of the planning period. The comparability of two countries in terms of skill and education patterns is highly questionable under

8

any circumstances, thus the basic assumption is weak. Moreover, this is another case of an approach based on "need," without assessment of benefits or opportunity costs.

The social demand approach to planning offers one way to formulate a general strategy of educational development. The strategy is based upon political consideration (for example, the desirability of universal primary education) or on aspirations to reach the status of some country chosen as an analog. These are not true strategies; they are more nearly arbitrary targets. In addition they have often proved infeasible, or even detrimental because they created stresses and distortions. There is a need to set forth a strategy for educational development, but this can and should be based on factors other than arbitrary assessments of social demand.

A number of computable models based upon input-output techniques have been developed.[22] These are largely mathematical statements of the two planning approaches above. They plot the quantitative development of the education system and permit identification of bottlenecks in its development. At best they can be used to indicate (very quickly if computerized) that implications of changes in major assumptions or policies on enrollment, teacher requirements, and costs. In this respect, such deterministic models are handy, but they do not aid the decision maker in knowing whether such changes are economically or socially beneficial. Nor do they cast any light on changes that might be made within any of the major components in the system to improve its effectiveness. Appendix C presents data from a simple computerized flow model developed by the writer for projecting enrollment growth in the Malaysian education system. Up to this point, the approaches described have been nonanalytical varieties of the quantitative projection method of planning.

Manpower Analysis

Manpower studies have been used to indicate needs for educated manpower in various developing countries. One of the earliest proponents of the approach was H. S. Parnes.[23] This idea has many supporters but it has also been severely criticized.[24] The principal points raised here will be critical ones, although there are ways in which relating the outputs of the education sector to employment opportunities in the economy is useful. The manpower analysis approach to education sector planning can be set forth in a few propositions.

Proposition 1. An important objective of the education system is to provide the educated manpower needed in order to achieve satisfactory growth of economic output. Humanistic critics argue that manpower analysts view this as the only objective. Economists argue somewhat differently that the estimates of "need" discussed below are of questionable validity, and that the economic benefits of producing educated graduates of various types should be measured against the costs of providing the education. Manpower analysts tend to view their estimates of requirements by education level as absolutes, regardless of benefits and costs. There is also nothing in the manpower approach that would indicate whether alternative means of providing the education needs might be preferable to existing educational practices. The only guidance offered to sectoral planners is on the numbers of graduates of each type that will be required.

Proposition 2. Educational "needs" are a function of employment by occupation; that is, there are fairly clear relationships between occupations and the education levels of the persons employed in them. These relationships amount to educational requirement coefficients by occupation. This proposition rests on the assumption that there is little or no substitutability between skills. While there are, to be sure, some relationships between education levels and occupations (especially for some technical specialties and professions requiring certification) it is also possible to observe a high degree of skill substitution in any portion of a labor force.* Although primary-school dropouts cannot be engineers, to cite an extreme case, it is entirely possible for a graduate from an "academic" high school to work at a skilled trade, or for a trained teacher to work as a dry goods clerk. This proposition also ignores the importance of on-job training as a source of highly skilled workmen, assuming that virtually all skills must be formally trained. This is one of the weakest points in the manpower approach. Its weakness is particularly evident when manpower planners attempt to work backward from occupational projections to estimates of education needs.

Measurement of the educational requirements coefficients is based on surveys of the employed labor force in the usual practice. Surveys of employment by economic sector by occupation by education level yield profiles of the educational distribution of the labor force. Here there are simple problems of measurement. Labor force data in developing countries are far less complete than in developed countries. Sampling and reporting errors may be magnified many times

---

*The assumption of low skill substitution affects the nature of the education and training provided. The higher the degree of skill substitution, the more general education can be. Very low substitutability implies that each worker must be specifically trained for his occupation.

and the classifications of workers' education and occupation are usually crude. In the end, however, manpower studies state that certain proportions of each occupation in each sector (for example, "craftsmen and production process workers" in the industrial sector) have various levels of education (expressed either in years of schooling or by level of education completed).

In addition to the problem of basic measurement there are serious problems that arise in attempting to project the future. The present educational profile of the labor force in a developing country is hardly a model for what is desired in the future, therefore some attempt is usually made to allow for general educational upgrading. This can be done either on the basis of arbitrary assumptions or by comparison with the education-by-occupation profiles in more advanced countries (or in the more modern firms in the same country). International comparisons offer a very weak and potentially misleading basis for estimation because of differences (even between countries with similar incomes per capita) in the supplies of education available and productive technologies. "Leading firm" comparisons may be somewhat better but have to be used with care and involve a substantial element of judgment.

Proposition 3. Employment by occupation is a function of total economic output by sector and changes in productivity in each sector; that is, you can project occupational distributions on the basis of projections of total sectoral output, adjusted for changes in output per employee. This means that manpower projections are only as strong as the underlying projections of output and estimates of productivity change. Such projections are frequently wide of the mark by a considerable margin. There are tendencies for output projections to be high (due to optimism, politics, and so on) and for labor productivity estimates to be low, both of which bias manpower estimates upward.

There are other difficulties that affect this proposition. It assumes that the occupational distribution of a sector's labor force will remain the same even though the sector is likely to experience significant technological change. This is at least questionable. And even if one can accept the productivity estimate arrived at for the sector, this is an average productivity figure that may obscure differences between productivity trends for different occupations. One assumes that the output estimates upon which manpower projections are based are expressed in constant prices, so that monetary increases in the value of sectoral output do not create an upward bias in the manpower estimates.

This proposition again raises problems of measurement. In this case the problems involve the employment and occupation estimates by sector. Employment and occupation surveys have limitations

11

of coverage. Most surveys cover large firms, the industrial sectors, and public employment fairly completely but are weak in their coverage of small enterprises and of the agricultural and commercial sectors. Often even the number of firms with fewer than five or ten employees is not known, so stratification of sample surveys is difficult. And in many developing countries, employment in noncommercial or smallholder agriculture is extremely large. It is, moreover, highly probably that there are systematic differences between the occupation and education distributions of covered and noncovered firms. These data problems are sometimes dealt with on the basis of assumptions (for example, assume four years of education for all agricultural smallholders). They can of course be overcome through more careful and extensive surveying, but only at very high cost.

Proposition 4. The net change in employment by occupation can be calculated by subtracting present employment by occupation (determined by establishment surveys of employers) from the projected occupational distribution (as determined in proposition 3 above). The problems affecting the determination of the two major quantities affect the reliability of the difference calculation.

Proposition 5. The sum of the net increase in employment by occupation plus estimated attrition from the labor force (for reasons of death, retirement, or other labor force withdrawals, also broken down by occupation) equals total demand for new entrants to the labor force. Thus if the employment growth figures show a net increase of x master carpenters and another y master carpenters are assumed to die or retire, there will be a need for x plus y master carpenters during the period (and implicitly the schools should train that many). This is a major source of upward bias in manpower estimates. They show net change in the full range of skills and translate these changes into education needs. Carpenters, to take this example, cannot be trained in vocational schools to enter the labor force as fully qualified "master" carpenters. Opportunities for new entrants to the labor force are not found at all levels of the skill hierarchy. In all but a few cases, recent graduates enter the labor force via a relatively low-skilled or "entry-level" job. They advance to higher positions via on-job learning and internal promotion.[25] Estimates of skill "needs" thus tend to be biased toward higher skills while employment opportunities are all in the lowest ranks of the hierarchy.

Proposition 6. The outputs of the education system (graduates by level plus dropouts) that are "needed" to attain the economic output targets are determined by multiplying the demand for new entrants in each occupation by the educational requirement coefficients for each occupation. In other words, the total number of each sort of graduates during the plan period should match the "need" for new entrants having the relevant education. If there are surpluses or shortfalls, enrollment should be adjusted to bring outputs into balance with needs. Various complexities enter the calculations here. One involves the estimated unemployment rate at the end of the plan period. The economic growth and productivity change projections on which manpower estimates are based may either aim at full employment targets or they may be varied to indicate the probable employment implications of alternative growth rates. In either event, manpower estimates must take account of the occupational and educational characteristics of workers who either: (1) cease to be unemployed, or (2) enter the labor force from previous nonparticipation status. Information on these groups is minimal, especially in developing countries, and another potential source of error enters the calculation.

The final inputs from a manpower study into the education sector plan are indications of how enrollments in different types and levels of education should be adjusted to create a balance between school leavers and manpower needs. The preceding comments underline the need to use such information with caution.

In addition to the problems discussed above, there is another shortcoming that affects manpower planning. Assume that a manpower plan indicated a shortage of, say, vocational graduates (a frequent finding given the biases of the approach toward high-skill needs). The only information provided concerns the quantitative shortfall. Further, given the usual level of aggregation, all an educational planner learns from a manpower study is that he needs to increase enrollment and the number of graduates from vocational school. He does not usually know from the aggregate figures whether the vocational graduates should be trained in one specialty (for example, metalwork or electronics) or another. Nor does he know whether the training should begin after the eighth grade or the tenth; whether it should be of one, two, or three years' duration; what balance between theoretical training in the classroom and practical training in workships is needed; and so on. These are questions that are of great importance to planners and administrators, yet national manpower studies of the usual sort provide no guidance here. The only variable on which they provide information is the number of graduates of each type that are needed and the enrollment required to produce those graduates.

There are uses for manpower information. To cite an example from Malaysia, enrollment in academic secondary education increased very rapidly in the late 1960s, producing a large number of school leavers with eleven years of traditional academic education. These school leavers (that is, those who failed to gain access to the university-preparatory level) had more academic education than they

13

needed to become laborers and semiskilled workers and had traditionally become clerks, office workers, commercial employees, and so
on. Manpower studies indicated that employment opportunities in
these occupations would be limited, amounting to only about 20 percent
of the number of graduates. Clearly there was a problem, but the
information available provided little guidance on what to do. Reducing
enrollment in academic secondary education would have run counter
to social pressure and national goals of increased access to secondary
education. A shift to other types of secondary education (for example,
enrollment in the science stream or in vocational education) was
indicated, but decision makers had very little else to go on. The manpower data were useful in a partial sense, identifying the problem in
terms not of absolute "needs" but rather of employment opportunities.
There was, however, a need for other sorts of information. This
question is discussed later in this study.

For questions such as this, and in areas such as professional
and technical training where the relationship between education and
occupations is much more clear and direct, manpower information
can provide useful insights. Different sorts of manpower studies,
focusing upon opportunities for new entrants to the labor force for
example, could be valuable; especially when used in conjunction with
other information such as investigation of the costs and benefits of
various types of education. But national level manpower planning,
as usually practiced, has serious weaknesses and provides information
on only a few variables (enrollment and graduates "needed").

Rate-of-Return Analysis

Of the most frequently used approaches to educational planning,
only rate-of-return analysis is based upon economic analysis. In
essence, rate-of-return analysis says that resources should be invested
in those types and levels of education that produce the greatest benefits in relation to their costs.* A complete technical explanation of

---

*Private rates of return are calculated on the basis of after-
tax earnings attributable to obtaining an additional increment of education and the out-of-pocket costs to the individual. Social rates of
return are based on before-tax income benefits and the total costs
to society of providing the schooling. Although private benefits and
costs provide useful information, public investment decisions are
based upon comparisons of social benefits and costs. Accepted practice now is to compare investments in terms of their internal rates
of return; that is, the rate of discount which, when applied to the

rate-of-return analysis is found in Gary Becker's <u>Human Capital</u>.[26]
This approach can be summarized in the propositions set forth below.

<u>Proposition 1</u>. Income is a function of workers' productivity and
wages tend to equal the marginal productivity of the worker. One
criticism of rate-of-return analysis is that wages often do not equal
marginal productivity but are instead "administered prices." This
may be especially true in developing countries where labor market
mechanisms do not function smoothly. For example, public sector
employment represents a large portion of total employment in many
developing countries, and wages tend to diverge more widely from
marginal productivity in public employment. Blaug lists other reasons
why wages may depart from marginal productivity: the role of family
connections, "snob value" associated with education, nepotism, entry
restrictions to some occupations, and so on.[27] He acknowledges
that there are many labor market imperfections, but argues that the
strong association observed between education and income is itself
evidence in favor of the marginal productivity assumption.[28] This
argument would seem to depend upon a relationship between education
and physical productivity, an area in which empirical evidence is very
limited. Blaug feels that the assumption is adequately justified, and
that rate-of-return calculations based upon observed wage rates are
valid. He does, however, admit that the arguments against this assumption "carry real force" in underdeveloped countries.[29]

<u>Proposition 2</u>. Education has an effect upon productivity, and im-
proving productivity (and earnings) is an important objective of educational policy. The arguments against this proposition are that
there are many benefits—personal, social, and external economic
benefits—that are not measured by income differences, and that these
are in fact more important than the directly observable income benefits. Some calculations of rates of return attempt to adjust for the
"consumption benefits" of education (for example, greater enjoyment
of life as a result of being educated), although the methods are fairly
arbitrary. Allowance for social benefits such as more effective citi-
zenship, lower birth rates, and so on, are difficult to make although
B. A. Weisbrod has explored the external benefits of education in
the United States.[30] There may also be external costs of education
in developing countries, as for example the strong relationships

----

lifetime benefit stream attributable to the education, equates the
benefits with the costs of the education. This criterion avoids the
problems of comparing projects of different scale and of the choice
of an appropriate discount rate.

between education and migration to already-overcrowded metropolitan areas. In general, external benefits outweigh external costs and thus tend to increase the rates of return. The existence of externalities casts some doubt, however, upon the precision of measurements of rates of return.

Proposition 3. There is a high degree of substitutability between different skills or different levels of education. In other words, persons will seek employment in occupations that offer the highest pay, even though they may not have been specifically trained for the new occupation. This assumption is exactly the opposite to the manpower approach's assumption of very low elasticity of substitution. The high-substitutability assumption conforms more closely to the realities of the labor market, although perfect elasticity is probably not achieved. Substitution of skills or of education takes place within relative ranges. A high-school graduate can perform a wide range of occupations around the middle level of the skill hierarchy but he is unlikely to dig ditches and unable to function as a certified professional in medicine, engineering, law, and so on.

Proposition 4. The economic benefits of education can be measured by the differences in average incomes between groups of persons with different education levels. That is to say, adding an increment of education (for instance, going to secondary school instead of stopping after primary school) results in greater income; and the difference between the lifetime earnings streams of persons with different education levels, discounted to present value, constitute the benefits to the added education. One of the most serious objections to rate-of-return analysis arises at this point. Observed income differentials are based upon the relative scarcities of different sorts of education in the labor market. If the supply of a given sort of education changes substantially, the earnings associated with it are also likely to change. In developing countries, where stocks of educated manpower are small and substantial changes in the outputs of different levels of education occur rapidly, the relative returns to different levels of education are especially subject to change. Rates of return observed from cross-sectional studies at a point in time reflect points on the demand curves for different sorts of education but do not indicate the slopes of these demand curves. The findings indicate that planners should allocate more resources to the higher-return forms of education but do not indicate how much more. One approach to this problem is to repeat the rate-of-return studies periodically in order to see how rates of return are changing.[31] C. R. S. Dougherty has addressed the problem in a linear programming model by calculating the elasticities of substitution of different sorts of education.[32] The

lower the elasticity, the more rapidly the rates of return are expected
to change in response to supply changes. His technique "takes into
account explicitly the diminishing returns effect of the growth of the
educational system on its own profitability."[33] This provides one
answer to the problem of projecting returns into the future. Other
problems relating to this proposition involve measurement difficulties
and problems of categorization and aggregation. Earnings data are
based upon large sample surveys of the population. The soundness
of the sampling techniques may be subject to question, particularly
in developing countries, and the costs of obtaining such data are high.
Sample surveys gather data on major categories of education (primary,
secondary, and so on) and do not provide detail on differences in
earnings between alternatives at the same level. (Another problem,
discussed below, is that no information is available regarding recently
implemented programs or totally new alternatives.) Greater detail
cannot ordinarily be provided because of limitations of statistical
reliability, thus the information produced relates only to broad categories of education. Such information is useful, to be sure, but its
use is limited.

Proposition 5. Investment in education should be concentrated on
those levels and types of education that have the highest rates of
return; that is, enrollment should be increased in the high-return
levels of education. This is the policy information that rate-of-return
planning yields. Like manpower planning, the only variable with
which it deals is enrollment. As noted above, educational planners
and administrations need information on many other variables. Because of a lack of detail, planners cannot use the data to indicate
which of various existing alternatives is most beneficial (for example,
traditional academic education vs. science and technical education
at the secondary level). Nor can the sorts of rate-of-return studies
usually applied provide information on recently implemented changes
or pilot programs. Some countries have experimented with comprehensive education, for example, but since there have been few
graduates and they have not been in the labor force long enough to
reveal the age-income profile resulting from such education, rate-of-
return analysis cannot, in its usual form, cast light upon the benefits
derived from such experimental programs. Many modifications could
be made in this planning approach to overcome some of its shortcomings. Blaug recognizes the need for such developments in the
approach:

> In the past, rate-of-return analysis has been almost
> exclusively concerned with evaluating the yield of extra
> years or levels of education. But analysis of different

amounts of education must be considered only a first
step in a more comprehensive approach which would
include the effects of various kinds of education.[34]

Unfortunately, he adds, little has been done in this area.

A PROBLEM OF ORIENTATION OF THE MAJOR APPROACHES

The preceding discussions of educational planning have been
critical of the most frequent applications of various approaches to
planning for educational development. The problems are of various
sorts. The main approaches—quantitative projections, manpower
analysis and rate-of-return analysis—often suffer from problems of
measurement and data inadequacies. Or their usual applications
have shortcomings because important factors are simply overlooked.
These problems could perhaps be overcome with better data, more
meaningful disaggregation, and more thorough attention to such matters
as the role of on-job learning or ways to predict the slopes of the
demand curves for categories of educated labor.

There are, however, other problems not so easily remedied.
These involve fundamental weaknesses in the well-known conceptual
frameworks for planning educational expenditures. Purely quantitative
projection of sectoral growth provides no guidance on the ways in
which education can contribute to national goals; only on how the system will grow if past trends continue. Adoption of arbitrary targets
without analysis, as in the social demand approach, does not solve
this problem. The manpower approach is based upon the questionable
assumption that the relationships between education and occupation
are clear and stable; that is, that substitution of skills takes place
only within very narrow limits. The rate-of-return approach, while
on a more sound theoretical footing than the others, addresses only
the economic or income objective of education. And because it is
based upon data from surveys of the existing labor force, it tends to
use average data for marginal decisions. Much of the literature on
educational planning has addressed the technical and conceptual problems of the approaches themselves, as has this discussion so far.
The many problems inherent in manpower and rate-of-return planning
have led knowledgeable observers to conclude: "Evidently both manpower and rate-of-return approaches have severe limitations."[35]

The argument advanced against the major approaches in this
study concerns a different set of problems. These involve the orientation of the approaches toward high-level reallocations of resources
between major types of education. Even under the best of circumstances,

18

assuming all technical and data problems could be overcome, planning
tools that only indicate whether to increase or decrease enrollment
in the various levels of education are of very limited interest to administrators concerned with efficiency and making education systems
work better. Consideration of benefits and costs, as in the rate-of-
return approach, is certainly not wrong (other, more useful applications
of benefit-cost analysis will be considered below), and even broad
assessment of manpower questions can be useful. But the information
outputs from existing planning approaches do not match the information
needs of decision makers as stated in the definition of planning. The
information produced does not indicate how well the system is accomplishing its goals or how the cost-effectiveness of such accomplishment could be improved.

One writer has described the tasks of planning and expenditure
analysis as asking, and answering, several questions. Where are
resources going? What is being accomplished with these resources?
How can the process of providing education be better accomplished?[36]
If these are the questions (and they relate closely to the definition of
planning used here), how well do the major planning approaches answer
them? In terms of indicating where resources are going, even quantitative projection planning has failed to provide adequate information
on educational costs and the distribution of costs within educational
budgets.[37] Manpower analysis largely ignores resource questions,
often indicating "needs" that would impose impossible cost burdens
if fully met. Rate-of-return analysis examines costs carefully, but
only as an element in the rate-of-return calculation.

What about the question of what is being accomplished with
available resources? The only criterion of accomplishment in manpower planning is the degree to which educational outputs match
occupational demands. Rate-of-return analysis does at least examine
the results of investments, but it does so only in terms of an income
objective and only in relation to large aggregates (that is, earnings
of graduates of some five to seven types of education). Its view of
accomplishment, or the effectiveness of resource use is thus very
narrow.

With regard to improving the effectiveness of educational investments—of doing the job better—only rate-of-return planning offers
any guidance. Its prescription for improving sectoral effectiveness
is to shift resources to those forms of education producing the highest
economic returns. In other words the main policy parameter with
which it deals is enrollment in different levels. This is theoretically
sound but from the standpoint of the working administrator, such
advice is sterile and narrow. The parameters of the system he
administers include not only the magnitude of enrollment but also
the supply and qualifications of teachers, alternative curricula,

internal organization and emphasis on subject materials, inputs of facilities and teaching materials, the costs of all these things, and so on. Planning approaches that provide guidance on manipulation of only one of these parameters may be useful (at least if one can believe their results), but they leave a great many resource allocation questions unanswered. This is why the major planning approaches fail to meet the information needs of administrators, and why a change in their orientation is urged.

If educational planning, which is supposed to guide expenditure decisions, fails to provide guidance on important allocation questions, where did it go wrong? Why are the major planning approaches oriented toward such a limited set of high-level decisions? The answer lies in part in the origins of education sector planning. Planning in most developing countries began at the national level, often at the urging of external lending agencies such as the World Bank or USAID. Macro-economic planning addressed problems of national growth, savings, investment, foreign exchange needs, price stability, and the balance between public and private sector activities in terms of large aggregates. When the broad dimensions of public investment were established, questions of allocation between various public sectors were addressed. The last questions to be asked involved intra-sectoral planning and project development. These were often the weakest elements in national planning, as Waterston has emphasized.[38]

Most education ministries carried on unsophisticated forms of quantitative projection planning prior to the advent of national planning. This provided no strategy or rationale for sectoral development, however, and the competing approaches of manpower and rate-of-return analysis were developed to provide some broad perspective on how the sector should develop in the long run. These approaches dealt with the interfaces between sectoral planning and national planning. Internal problems of implementation and internal efficiency were left to technicians and specialists within the sectoral planning offices. Unfortunately the application of economic science to the education sector seemed to stick at this point. The attention of able economists was distracted by the controversy between manpower and rate-of-return planning—two ways of looking at the same, high-level questions. The rapture of linear programming models, which still dealt in large aggregates, further absorbed the talents of economists. A brief flurry of interest in educational production functions seemed to herald an interest in efficiency decisions within the sector and in the parameters with which educational administrators were seriously concerned.[39] A number of problems specific to education—notably, lack of understanding of the "production process" and inability to specify inputs or outputs clearly—led to disaffection with production function analysis, although a number of researchers continue this line of inquiry.[40] (See Appendix B of this book for a discussion of one production function study.) In general, then, analysis of expenditure decisions in the education sector has approached the subject from the top down, avoided questions of the internal efficiency of the sector, and addressed a limited set of parameters.

The state of the art of public expenditure analysis has advanced rapidly in the developed countries, particularly in the areas of defense and water resources planning. Systems analysis and program budgeting brought an economic perspective to expenditure choices in unlikely and widely differing substantive areas. Application of these tools in the education sector and in developing countries, however, has lagged. In part this is due to preoccupation with macro-oriented planning approaches. And in part it is due to scarcity of data on which to base lower-level economic analysis and to inherent difficulties of analyzing educational performance. But it is entirely possible to apply economic analysis to the education sector in more fruitful ways than has been done in the past. The techniques are available (one of them is benefit-cost analysis, which underlies the rate-of-return approach). Data can be generated through different sorts of policy research that will provide a basis for analyses of significant policy questions. What is needed is a shift in orientation from the concentration on macro-allocation questions dealing only with the enrollment parameter, to the full range of expenditure analysis questions: Where are resources going? What is being accomplished? How can the various parts of the education sector be made to work somewhat better than at present?

NOTES

1. The distinction between discipline-oriented and problem-oriented economists is taken from G. F. Papanek, Development Policy: Theory and Practice (Cambridge: Harvard University Press, 1968), pp. 345-59.

2. R. Stone, Mathematics in the Social Sciences and Other Essays (London: Chapman and Hall, 1966), pp. 33-40.

3. See, for example, C. R. Dechert, ed., The Social Impact of Cybernetics (Notre Dame, Ind.: University of Notre Dame Press, 1966). For a more recent view of the subject area, see E. S. Dunn, Economic and Social Development: A Process of Social Learning (Baltimore: Johns Hopkins University Press, 1971). Part IV presents a review of converging bodies of thought.

4. C. E. Beeby assumes a close interrelationship between the two in his thoughtful essay, Planning and the Educational Administrator (Paris: UNESCO, Fundamentals of Education Planning Series, No. 4, 1967), pp. 34-35.

5. See, for example, Kjell Eide, "Organization of Education Planning," in D. Adams, ed., Educational Planning (Syracuse, N.Y.: Syracuse University Press, 1964), pp. 67-81.

6. C. A. Anderson and M. J. Bowman tend toward this view in their well-known article, "Theoretical Considerations in Educational Planning," in Adams, op. cit., pp. 4-46.

7. A. O. Hirschman and C. E. Lindblom, "Economic Development, Research and Development, Policy Making: Some Converging Views," Behavioral Science 7 (1962): 211-22; reprinted in F. E. Emery, ed., Systems Thinking (Middlesex, England: Penguin, 1969), pp. 351-71.

8. C. J. Hitch, The Uses of Economics (Santa Monica: RAND Corporation, 1960), address given at the Center for Advanced Study, Brookings Institute, Washington, D.C.; November 17, 1960.

9. Anderson and Bowman, op. cit.

10. Y. Dror, "The Planning Process," International Review of Administrative Sciences (Brussels) 29, no. 1 (1963): 50-52; Cited in Anderson and Bowman, op. cit., p. 5.

11. Anderson and Bowman, op. cit., p. 6.

12. Ibid.

13. Ibid., p. 8. For a theoretical statement of the shortcomings of the optimality criterion, see R. G. Lipsey and K. Lancaster, "The General Theory of Second Best," Review of Economic Studies 24 (1956): 11-32.

14. Anderson and Bowman, op. cit., p. 9.

15. Adams, ed., 1964, op. cit., pp. 67-81.

16. Ibid., p. 80.

17. Beeby, op. cit., p. 9.

18. Two survey articles that review the several approaches are: M. J. Bowman, "Economics of Education," Review of Educational Research 39, no. 5: 641-70; and H. M. Phillips, "Education and Development," Investment in Education (Bangkok: UNESCO Regional Office for Education in Asia, 1967), pp. 255-98. Detailed discussion of the manpower and rate-of-return approaches to planning are found in M. Blaug, An Introduction to the Economics of Education (London: Allen Lane The Penguin Press, 1970), pp. 137-68 and 200-34.

19. J. D. Chesswas, Methodologies for Educational Planning for Developing Countries (Paris: UNESCO International Institute for Educational Planning, 1969).

20. Phillips, op. cit., pp. 266 ff.

21. Ibid.

22. See, for example, the following sources: G. B. Kleindorfer and L. M. S. Roy, "A Model for Educational Planning in East Pakistan" (Dacca: Pakistan-Berkeley Program in Educational Planning, Ford Foundation, 1969); G. B. Kleindorfer, M. D. White, and C. S. Benson,

"A Planning and Implementation Model for Vocational Education,"
(Pakistan-Berkeley Program in Education Planning, Ford Foundation,
1970); C. A. Moser and P. Redfern, "Education and Manpower: Some
Current Research," in Models for Decision (London: The English
Universities Press, 1964); Stone, op. cit., Ch. IV; UNESCO, An Asian
Model of Educational Development (Paris: 1966).

    23. H. S. Parnes, "Manpower Analysis in Educational Planning,"
and "Relation of Occupation to Educational Qualification," in Parnes,
ed., Planning Education for Economic and Social Development (Paris:
OECD, 1964), reprinted in M. Blaug, ed., Economics of Education: 1
(Middlesex: Penguin, 1968), pp. 263-86. The approach was applied
under the auspices of the OECD in six member countries and in
Argentina and Peru. See R. G. Hollister, "A Technical Evaluation
of the OECD's Mediterranean Regional Project and Conclusions,"
in The World Yearbook of Education: 1967, J. A. Lauwerys, G. Z.
Bereday and M. Blaug, eds., reprinted in Blaug, Economics of Education: 2. For additional reference, see Manpower Aspects of Educational Planning (Paris: UNESCO/IIEP, 1968).

    24. Anderson and Bowman, op. cit.; M. Blaug, "The Rate of
Return on Investment in Education in Great Britain," The Manchester
School 33, no. 3 (1965): 205-51, reprinted in Blaug, Economics of
Education: 1.

    25. P. B. Doeringer and M. Piore, "Labor Market Adjustment
and Internal Training," Industrial Relations Research Association,
Proceedings of the Eighteenth Annual Meeting, pp. 1-14.

    26. G. Becker, Human Capital (New York: Columbia University
Press, 1964), pp. 33-67. See also Blaug, An Introduction to the Economics of Education, op. cit., pp. 54-60.

    27. Blaug, An Introduction to the Economics of Education, op.
cit., p. 206.

    28. Ibid., p. 207.

    29. Ibid., p. 209.

    30. B. A. Weisbrod, External Benefits of Public Education:
An Economic Analysis (Princeton: Princeton University Press,
1964).

    31. Samuel Bowles, "Efficient Allocation of Resources in Edu-
cation," in H. Chenery, ed., Studies in Development Planning (Cambridge: Harvard University Press, 1971), p. 251.

    32. C. R. S. Dougherty, "Optimal Allocation of Investment in
Education," in Chenery, op. cit., pp. 270-92.

    33. Ibid., p. 290.

    34. Blaug, An Introduction to the Economics of Education, op.
cit., p. 233.

    35. Anderson and Bowman, op. cit., cited in Blaug, An Intro-
duction to the Economics of Education, op. cit., p. 216.

36. Adapted from A. M. Rivlin, "The Planning, Programming and Budgeting System in the Department of Health, Education and Welfare: Some Lessons from Experience," in R. H. Haveman and J. Margolis, eds., Public Expenditure and Policy Analysis (Chicago: Markham, 1971), p. 502.

37. P. H. Coombs and J. Hallak, Managing Educational Costs (New York: Oxford University Press, 1972).

38. Albert Waterston, Development Planning—Lessons from Experience (Baltimore: Johns Hopkins Press, 1965).

39. Samuel Bowles, "Towards an Educational Production Function," in W. Lee Hansen, ed., Education and Income, Conference on Research on Income and Wealth (Princeton: Princeton University Press, 1970), pp. 55-78.

40. H. M. Levin, "A New Model of School Effectiveness" in U.S. Department of Health, Education and Welfare, Office of Education, Do Teachers Make a Difference? (Washington, D.C.: Government Printing Office, 1970), pp. 55-78.

Library
I.U.P.
Indiana, Pa.

379.5951 M227e
C.1

**IMPROVING EXPENDITURE
ANALYSIS IN THE
EDUCATION SECTOR**

It cannot be stated too frequently or emphasized enough
that economic choice is a way of looking at problems
and does not necessarily depend upon the use of any
analytic aids or computational devices.

C. J. Hitch and R. N. McKean[1]

The role of planning—whether in defense, water resources
policy, or education—is to provide information to decision makers
about allocating fiscal and other resources. The process of analyzing
public expenditure choices has emerged as a major branch of economics only in relatively recent years.[2] The central element in public expenditure analysis is benefit-cost analysis. This analytical tool
involves the comparison of the total benefits of an investment (appro-
priately discounted to present value) with the present value of total
costs.[3] This, it will be recalled, is the concept underlying the rate-
of-return approach to educational planning. Since it measures benefits in economic terms, benefit-cost analysis is useful only in cases
where benefits are monetary or can be converted to money terms.
This is a serious limitation in analyzing social sector expenditures
such as education.

Because of this limitation, a modification of the concept, called
cost-effectiveness analysis, was developed. Much of the literature
on cost-effectiveness analysis concerns its applications in defense
analyses, where it originated.[4] Blaug compares benefit-cost and
cost-effectiveness analysis in the education sector.[5] Cost-effectiveness
permits comparing costs with the outputs or results of an investment,
even though these cannot be readily expressed in terms of money.
This is done either by setting quantitative output goals and attempting
to find the least-cost method of achieving the desired output, or by
maximizing output subject to a fixed budgetary constraint. If, for

example, 300 qualified secondary science teachers were needed, alternative training programs would be compared in order to see which was the most efficient way of training the teachers. Or, if a given budget were available for secondary science teacher training, programs could be compared to see which would produce the most teachers with the funds available.

As noted in Chapter 1, this concept of getting the most for your money seems simple, but it is not a generally recognized mode of considering expenditure choices in the education sector. It is, however, a powerful tool and a fundamental ingredient of economic analysis of educational investment choices. Because it can be used to analyze programs producing nonmonetary benefits (for example, gains in academic performance), its range of applicability is much broader than benefit-cost analysis. Other modifications on the basic concept of comparing the benefits derived from an expenditure with the costs are variously called cost-utility or resource-effectiveness analysis and do not differ significantly from cost-effectiveness as described here.

Systems analysis is a somewhat more elaborate approach to analyzing complex policy questions.[6] It is based on the quantitative techniques of economics—notably benefit-cost and cost-effectiveness analysis—and of operations research, and was largely developed for analysis of defense expenditure questions. (The standard work on military systems analysis is by C. J. Hitch and R. N. McKean.)[7] A system can be loosely defined as a set of interrelated activities leading to a goal. Systems analysis, however, is more difficult to define. It originally involved the use of complex mathematical models, often with the aid of computers. A system or "package" of activities relating to a particular task (for example, a defense weapons system) is identified. The characteristics of the system are expressed as mathematical functions. Mathematical models of system performance, often incorporating the optimizing techniques of linear programming, are developed to determine the best combinations of inputs. Costs are estimated and the choice between alternative systems is based upon their relative cost-effectiveness.

As the quantitative techniques of systems analysis were applied to higher policy questions with more than one goal or with less measurable goals, the scarcity of data and the complexity of dealing with multiple goals limited the use of mathematical models. It was found, however, that the principles of carefully structuring the policy questions asked and comparing alternative programs or systems in terms of their contributions to goals could be usefully applied, even though mathematical models could not. Clay Whitehead provides a balanced discussion of systems analysis and its role in administrative decision making.[8]

It is frequently suggested that systems analysis be brought to bear upon nonmilitary problems, particularly public sector investment decisions where the test of market competition does not automatically lead to efficiency.[9] Applications in the education sector have also been suggested.[10] This idea is opposed by many people who associate systems analysis with (fallible) military expenditure analysis and "management by computer." There is room for skepticism about how far systems analysis of a highly quantitative sort can be applied in education. But the underlying principles of determining what outputs are desired, measuring performance, and comparing alternatives in terms of costs and effectiveness constitute a useful "way of looking at problems."

An interesting distinction between benefit-cost, cost-effectiveness and systems analysis is drawn by Guy Black:

> The differences between cost-benefit analysis, cost-effectiveness analysis and microeconomic system analysis are that the first two are primarily means of evaluating proposals for given systems designs, whereas systems analysis treats the design parameters not as given but to be chosen.[11]

Still another conceptual framework for analyzing public expenditure decisions is program budgeting.[12] Rising public spending in almost all countries has created a need for better budgeting techniques.[13] Performance budgeting introduces the concept of relating expenditures to clearly identifiable activities or functional programs (as opposed to specific items of expenditure) and attempting to determine what the results of the programs are. The most elaborate development of this concept is program budgeting or Programming, Planning and Budgeting Systems (PPBS). It involves organizing the various agency or departmental activities in the budget into major categories or programs that relate to fairly discrete, identifiable functions. Objectives are established for each program. Outputs are identified in terms of those objectives, and attempts are made to quantify the outputs and relate them to costs. The full costs of an investment over a period of years are considered, rather than the annual increments to cost, so that decision makers can compare total benefits with total costs.

The basic tools of program budgeting are, once again, benefit-cost and cost-effectiveness analysis. The similarities between program budgeting and systems analysis are so great that many observers consider the two terms to be synonymous, and it is clear that both proceed from the same basic premises. Insofar as there are valid distinctions between the two, they are in their subject matter and scope. Program budgeting looks at the whole range of public expenditures at once, identifies objectives and performance, and allocates funds between proposed programs on the basis of relative costs and outputs. Systems analysis is more likely to be applied in developing the individual programs to be submitted for budget approval. It looks intensively at single, integrated systems rather than at the full array of programs making up a budget. Instead of choosing between already developed alternatives as budget analysts do, systems analysts are actively engaged in the design of the system and even in modification of the original goals.

A major move to apply program budgeting or PPBS in all agencies of the U.S. government was initiated by presidential directive in 1966. This move has been highly controversial. Quantitative analytical techniques are more readily adaptable in some fields than in others, so the success of PPBS has been uneven.[14] Some critics have argued that the procedural requirements of PPBS impose heavy burdens on agency administrators, that resistance to PPBS has led to merely token compliance that does not improve the budgeting process, and that the net effect of the PPBS movement has not been greatly beneficial. An articulate argument for less concern with the procedures of PPBS and more attention to careful policy analysis of relatively few critical expenditure decisions is advanced by Aaron Wildavsky.[15] Application of program budgeting in the education sector has been strongly recommended by at least one author.[16] Some countries have begun to convert their education budgeting process to a program budgeting format, but resistance and difficulties have been encountered. Despite difficulties that are real and some valid criticisms, program budgeting constitutes a major improvement over earlier, "line-item" budgeting methods.

One can draw subtle distinctions between these tools for analyzing expenditure choices but it is clear that all are based upon the same "way of looking at problems." All are concerned with making the most efficient use of available resources that is possible. All involve evaluating the effects or performance that result from an investment and comparing those effects with the costs incurred. And all operate by calculating the benefits and costs of alternative ways of performing a task and providing decision makers with information on which to base choices between the alternatives. The elements of economic analysis that underlie these tools are, then, the following:

1. Clarification of the objective or objectives for which the expenditure is made;

2. Identification of alternative ways of accomplishing this objective (that is alternative projects or activities) between which decision makers can choose;

3. Quantitative measurement or estimation of the performance and costs of each alternative; including, insofar as possible, measurement of external benefits and uses of resources;

4. Using the most suitable analytical tools at hand (benefit-cost, cost-effectiveness or related analytical techniques) to compare the alternatives; and

5. Presentation of the findings of the analysis to decision makers—who may either make a decision, reconsider the original objectives, revise the budget and call for further analysis, or otherwise make use of the information.[17]

The very brief discussion of the tools of expenditure analysis presented here overlooks several important qualifying factors. First there are many theoretical fine points and problems such as the proper way to discount future benefits, the measurement of external benefits and costs, and the choice of an appropriate criterion for choice that complicate the actual use of these tools.[18] Second, there are numerous practical problems such as identifying the true objectives of multidimensional programs, obtaining the data needed to perform the analysis and structuring the questions for decision in a clear fashion that permits analysis. An earlier work prepared by the writer considers some of these problems in the context of educational planning at length.[19] Finally, decisions tend to be made not in a straightforward and logical fashion—as the preceding discussions would suggest—but rather in an unstructured, iterative, or "political" way. The literature on the nonsystematic nature of the decision-making process is extensive.[20] The limitations on the use of economic analysis are important in developing countries generally and in the education sector in particular, as will be discussed below. It is not the intention of this study to minimize the problems of doing good policy analysis for developing education systems. It is a major purpose of the study, however, to indicate that an economic perspective on educational expenditure choices can offer far more useful policy guidance than the much discussed approaches to educational planning that have dominated the literature on and the practice of educational planning.

CHANGING THE ORIENTATION OF PLANNING

Suggesting that familiar tools such as cost-effectiveness analysis be applied to policy decisions in the education sector is hardly a radical conceptual departure. Yet there are important changes in the planning process implied. Planning and expenditure analysis in the education sector in developing countries have lagged far behind the state of the art in other areas. The definition of educational planning offered in

Chapter 1 seems innocuous, yet it represents a major departure from planning practice in most ministries of education throughout the developing world. Let us consider several ways in which the orientation of planning and expenditure analysis can be shifted away from the usual planning approaches and made more compatible with that definition.

Planning and the Hierarchy of Decisions

The definition of planning stresses its role in providing information for decision makers on how well the education system is accomplishing its goals and how the cost-effectiveness of such accomplishment can be improved. The discussion of the major planning approaches in the preceding chapter revealed, however, that these approaches offer information on only a limited set of goals (economic returns or manpower objectives) and provide guidance on only one policy instrument: altering enrollment levels in different categories of education to accomplish the goals. There has been a strong tendency to plan developing educational systems in this manner because of the relationship between education sector planning and central economic planning (discussed above), limited analytical expertise, and acute scarcity of data that would permit other sorts of analyses.

What should be the subject of economic analysis in education if not the allocation of resources to different levels and types of education? To answer this question, it will be useful to present two concepts: optimization and the hierarchy of policy decisions.

An optimum means an arrangement of circumstances that is unequivocally the best that can be achieved. Choice of an optimal investment means selection of the best, from which any departure would involve a sacrifice in terms of some objective. Given the complexities of the real world and of human institutions generally, identification of optimal, or even "second-best" solutions to problems is not a feasible pursuit.[21] The concept of seeking the best allocation of resources gives rise to a related idea—the "level of optimization" or the point on an hierarchy of decisions at which choices are made. Choices made at the highest level, in terms of the ultimate goals of society, are called "optimizing" choices; those made at lower levels in terms of goals that are themselves means to ultimate ends are called "suboptimizations."

The decisions made in an education ministry can be viewed as an hierarchy, although a strict hierarchical ranking does not exist and decisions may be taken in a more or less random order. The full hierarchy of public expenditure decisions, ranging downward through sectoral decisions, can be shown for the education sector as follows:

1. Choices between public and private uses of resources (that is, of the appropriate total tax burden);

2. Choices between public expenditures on social welfare programs on the one hand and other public programs (such as promoting economic growth and providing defense) on the other;

3. Choices within the social welfare "budget" between total expenditures on health, education, housing, and other welfare activities;

4. Choices within the education "budget" between expenditures on different levels and types of education (for example, primary, secondary, vocational, teacher training, and so on);

5. Choices within each level between expenditures on intralevel alternatives (for example, between arts and science stream schools, between vocational schools of different sorts or offering different specialties, or between primary and secondary teacher training);

6. Choices between different inputs into any given type of education (for example, teachers, textbooks, classroom space, laboratory facilities, libraries, and so on).[22]

If choices at the top level of the hierarchy are not optimal or "best" in terms of some social welfare criterion, then choices at lower levels will all depart to some degree from the best possible allocations. Since decision makers cannot be expected to consider the whole range of decisions at once, the usual practice in sectoral planning is to take the choices made at higher levels as given and make the best decisions one can within the budget allocated from above. That is, one suboptimizes, breaking down enormously complex sets of interrelated decisions into manageable subproblems and dealing with each in terms of its immediate context and objectives.

Suboptimization may be considered undesirable because it can lead to situations where lower-level activities (that is, means to achieving higher ends) take precedence over the higher-level goals themselves. In practice, however, suboptimization often turns out to be the only feasible way to analyze complex problems. This is especially true where ultimate goals are imperfectly understood and difficult to measure, as is the case in the education sector. Hitch and McKean point out the reasons for suboptimizations:

> Piecemeal analysis and decision making have great advantages . . . . Small problems tend to become more 'manageable' in a number of senses. As problems are broken down into smaller chunks, more detail can be taken into account by both researchers and decision-makers. In analysis . . . the models used in estimating outcomes can be less aggregative and more precise . . . than global models would be.[23]

There are, on the other hand, dangers inherent in suboptimization, as the same authors emphasize:

> The danger is that the criteria adopted in lower-level problems may be unrelated to and inconsistent with higher level criteria . . . . A whole hierarchy of proximate criteria comes into play and potential inconsistencies are abundant.[24]

Let us now consider the relationship between optimization, hierarchical decisions and approaches to educational planning. Educational planning decisions need to be taken at many levels of the hierarchy. The highest decisions dealt with by sectoral planners are at Level 3 in the hierarchy shown above: choice of the size of the education budget. Although this decision is largely imposed externally by national planners and the Treasury, education plans have some limited bearing upon it.* The next highest decisions are at Level 4: allocations between different types of education. Such decisions involve the relative growth of enrollment in each form of education, and it is toward this level of optimization that the major planning approaches are oriented. While such decisions are important, looking only at these turns economic analysis away from many critical choices at lower levels. Yet the major planning approaches do not provide insight into decisions below Level 4.

It is not wrong to provide information on Level 4 choices, but economic analysis can also do much more. It can even be argued that quantitative analytical tools are more powerful at lower levels than higher on the scale. Decisions at Levels 5 and 6, between intra-level alternatives and between expenditures on different sorts of inputs, are important. The case study presented in Chapters 4 and 5 illustrates the nature of such decisions and ways that economic analysis can cast light upon them. These lower-level decisions are numerically more frequent than Level 4 choices. Educational planners make major strategic choices about the growth of enrollment (and conduct manpower and rate-of-return studies) only every five years or so. But intrasector decisions arise continually and call for analysis.

The lower-level choices are also economically important, involving large investments and perhaps materially affecting the performance of educational programs. And decisions on enrollment

---

*Availability of prepared investment projects is a necessary justification for budget allocations to education, and indications of high rates of return relative to the opportunity cost of capital may be persuasive when arguing for more resources for the sector.

levels are inextricably related to lower-level choices—a serious point that is overlooked in the major planning approaches. If a manpower study shows that a surplus of, say, vocational graduates will be produced, policy can either: (1) limit enrollment in that stream, or (2) change the nature of the stream to improve the employability and earnings of its graduates. In another example of the relationship between lower-level and higher-level choices—if the rate of return to a given level of education is low, actions that reduce the costs of the education (without altering graduates' earning power) will increase the rates of return. The major planning approaches tend to assume that the types of education they manipulate are fixed. Working administrators recognize that they are not and need guidance on how to make individual programs more cost-effective. These are suboptimizing choices. Educational planning efforts have not, in practice, provided information on how to make them. Modifications in manpower and rate-of-return planning and introduction of other tools from the expenditure analysis kit are feasible and needed.

Planning as a Continuous Process

Planning in most ministries of education has not been conceived of as a "continuous process of providing information to decision makers" (as defined in Chapter 1), but rather as a one-way process leading to preparation of a plan document. The linear nature of the major planning approaches, as usually applied, is shown in block diagram form in Figure 2.1. While preparation of a plan document is a useful outgrowth of the continuous process of analyzing policy choices, it is far from the only function of educational planning.

It could be argued that manpower and rate-of-return analysis might be reapplied frequently so as to feed new information back into the decision-making process. In practice they have not been so applied, and it is probable that they cannot be in their usual forms. The reasons are as follows:

1. Measurements of aggregate manpower supply and requirements of average earnings by education level in the total labor force are not sensitive instruments for assessing the effectiveness of specific programs. Their categorization schemes are crude, marginal information is blurred by broad averages, and the costs of repeated broad surveys are high. (Modifications of the approaches may tend to overcome some of these problems; and that, in part, is what is advocated here.)

2. Enrollment decisions are not made frequently and, once made, have a tendency to be difficult to change.[25] Once classroom

33

FIGURE 2.1

Block Diagrams of Planning Approaches

Quantitative Projection Approach to Planning

Project growth of enrollment based on past trends or estimates of social demand → Calculate the facilities, teacher requirements, etc., needed to provide for growth → Prepare projects and estimate costs required to provide for projected growth

The Manpower Approach

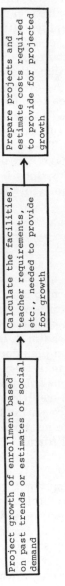
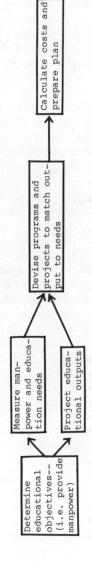

Determine educational objectives--(i.e. provide manpower) → Measure manpower and education needs / Project educational outputs → Devise programs and projects to match output to needs → Calculate costs and prepare plan

The Rate-of-Return Approach

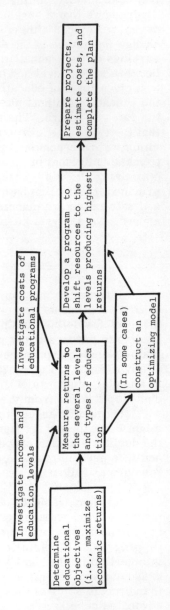

Determine educational objectives (i.e., maximize economic returns) → Investigate income and education levels / Investigate costs of educational programs → Measure returns to the several levels and types of education → Develop a program to shift resources to the levels producing highest returns → Prepare projects, estimate costs, and complete the plan

(In some cases) construct an optimizing model

space has been built and teachers trained to accommodate a planned enrollment increase, "retooling" of such physical and human capital is difficult.

 3. As noted, the variables on which the major approaches provide information are not the ones that affect the more frequent intrasectoral choices.

 Albert Waterston has noted that, despite general lip service paid to flexibility in planning and frequent revision, most planners in developing countries have not understood the need for continuous revision and iteration.[26] The reasons, he notes, include general inertia, lack of capability to carry out frequent replanning efforts, the lack of psychological appeal of a continuously revised plan in comparison with "new" medium term plans.* The usual approaches to educational planning do not lend themselves to continuous, flexible planning. Changing the orientation of economic analysis in the education sector toward evaluation of the observable outputs of specific programs would result in a planning approach that is much more flexible and suited to revision. As noted in Chapter 1, the conception of planning as advocated here is of a cybernetic process in which feedback of information leads to program adjustments and improved effectiveness. Additional benefits include a closer link with the annual budgeting process and greater familiarity on the part of administrators with the use of data and analysis for frequent program choices.

 The use of economic analysis on a continuing basis, as proposed here, can be diagrammed in a different fashion, as in Figure 2.2. This contrasts with the straight-line approaches of Figure 2.1. Major differences between the two include the circular nature of the process (with feedback from the implementation phase), the explicit search for new alternatives and the close link with the budgetary process. These differences may seem superficial but they represent a fundamental change in the usual practice of educational planning.

 Such an approach does not do away with periodic plans that delineate strategy for a period of years. Preparation of a plan document still serves to focus and formalize the ongoing process of analyzing policy decisions and is itself an important activity. The completed

---

 *Waterson discusses "rolling plans" (pp. 139-41). These are medium-term plans that are updated annually to take account of new information or changed circumstances. Puerto Rico has a successful Six Year Financial Program. The Philippines, the USSR, and the Union of South Africa have experimented with rolling plans, not always with success. Rolling plans would be a natural outgrowth of the continuous planning process diagrammed below.

FIGURE 2.2

Planning in a Continuous Process of Managing
Education Systems

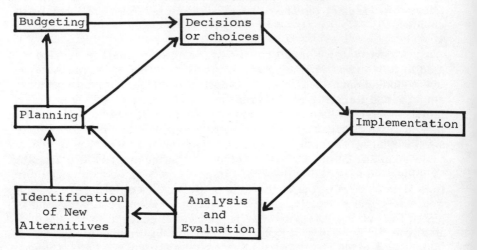

document serves as a guide for implementation during the plan's time
period. But the planning approach set forth here is more concerned
with the process of providing information to improve decisions than
with the crystalization of a set of decisions into a medium- or long-
term plan.

Efficiency in the Large and Efficiency in the Small

Efficiency is a concept with several facets. One can speak of
efficiency in the selection of goods to be produced, in the allocation
of resources in the production of the goods, and in the distribution of
goods among consumers.[27] Similar distinctions can be drawn between
kinds of efficiency in the production of educational services. P. H.
Coombs and J. Hallak distinguish between "internal efficiency" and
"external productivity" in education:

> Internal efficiency is the relationship between a system's
> outputs and the corresponding inputs that went into pro-
> ducing them.
> An education system's external producitvity is the
> relationship between the cumulative benefits derived
> from it over a given period and the corresponding inputs

36

used earlier (i. e. the cost or "investment" incurred) in producing these benefits.[28]

External productivity, as these authors define it, can be analyzed in benefit-cost terms while internal efficiency questions are generally subject to cost-effectiveness analysis. Once again we see a distinction between the subject area toward which the major planning approaches are oriented and another important area for efficiency analysis. Manpower and rate-of-return analysis consider external productivity questions or the efficient selection of the kinds of education to be produced. Thus a significant field for efficiency analysis is not covered by these approaches—questions of internal effectiveness or the allocation of resources in the production of education—even though the tools for such analysis are available. Coombs and Hallak, whose work focuses upon problems of cost measurement as illustrated in 27 cases drawn from throughout the developing and developed world, find that: "Even in the most highly-industrialized countries, educational systems have not been very 'cost-conscious' in the sense of analyzing their costs for purposes of evaluation, planning, policy-making and general improvement of their cost-effectiveness."[29] In other words planners and economists have not been asking and answering efficiency questions.

An innovative insight into the question of efficiency is advanced by Harvey Leibenstein, who distinguishes between allocative efficiency as usually considered by economists and "X-efficiency."[30] Microeconomic theory assumes that productive units combine inputs or resources so as to operate on a production possibility frontier, that is, that the internal technical process of production is efficient. Gains in allocative efficiency are achieved by moving along the production possibility frontier (altering the output mix) to a point of tangency with the highest utility curve, as shown by a move from m to n along the frontier F in Figure 2.3.

Leibenstein's findings, based upon empirical data from industrial firms that experienced substantial changes in productivity, suggest that productive units "do not operate on an outer-bound production possibility surface consistent with their resources."[31] Instead their outputs are less than they might be, given available resources, as at point k in Figure 2.3. A move from m to n constitutes a gain in allocative efficiency; a move from k to n, a gain in X-efficiency.

> For a variety of reasons people and organizations work
> neither as hard nor as effectively as they could. In situa-
> tions where competitive pressure is light, many people
> will trade the disutility of greater effort, of search, and
> the control of other peoples' activities for the utility of

FIGURE 2.3

X-Efficiency and Allocative Efficiency Gains
in Production

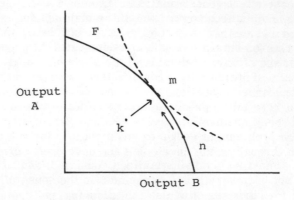

feeling less pressure and of better interpersonal relations. But in situations where competitive pressures
are high, they will exchange less of the disutility of
effort for the utility of freedom from pressure, etc . . . .
The data suggest that the amount to be gained by increasing allocative efficiency is trivial while the
amount to be gained by increasing X-efficiency is frequently significant.[32]

Leibenstein found that allocative efficiency gains in the private
sector might be on the order of 0.001 to 1.0 percent while X-efficiency
improvements resulting from technical changes, better waste control,
worker training, and changes in work method resulted in unit cost
reductions ranging from 5.0 to 83.0 percent.[33]

If the concept of X-efficiency is of demonstrable importance in
the private sector, where monetary profits serve as a clear indicator
of performance and an incentive to improve efficiency, then it is likely
that X-inefficiency is even more important in the public sector and
especially in the education field. Educational performance is difficult
to measure and relate back to the specific inputs in the production
process and the incentive system for teachers and school administrators is only indirectly related to performance. Data presented in
Chapter 4 indicate that there are apparently substantial differences
in educational performance (as measured by longitudinal gains on

examination scores), even when one controls for levels of inputs in either quantitative or cost terms, in Malaysian secondary schools. Chapter 5 shows glaring inefficiencies in a vocational program that continued unnoticed (and were even defended). Economic analysis can provide information that leads to X-efficiency improvements. But decisions affecting X-efficiency arise at Levels 5 and 6 on the decision hierarchy, where manpower and rate-of-return analysis offer virtually no information. (The analytical tool that is most appropriate for analysis of X-efficiency is cost-effectiveness analysis, which can incorporate nonmonetary variables.) The standard planning approaches assume efficiency of the production processes between which they allocate resources. They are therefore ill-suited exploration of this phenomenon. The need to investigate the effectiveness of educational production processes is an important reason for changing the orientation of educational planning.*

ELEMENTS OF ECONOMIC ANALYSIS OF EDUCATION: SOME PROBLEMS

Earlier portions of this chapter have considered the major analytical tools or frameworks for analyzing expenditure choices: benefit-cost, cost-effectiveness and system analysis, plus program budgeting. It has been suggested that a synthesis of the main elements of these tools be used to provide an economic perspective on educational expenditure choices. The differences between such a synthesized approach to expenditure analysis and the major approaches to planning have been identified: differences in terms of continuousness, orientation toward a broader range on the decision hierarchy, and focus upon the internal effectiveness of educational systems. What are the problems involved in applying these methodologies and this orientation to the education sector in developing countries? There are many problems but, as will be discussed, they are not totally insuperable; and the effort to overcome them is worthwhile.

---

*As noted above, attempts to identify educational production functions have failed to establish clear relationships between inputs and performance and have been criticized as futile given the non-specificity of inputs, outputs, and the production process in education. It is interesting to speculate that the problems of production function studies might be due to existence of large (even huge) X-inefficiencies. Their existence would violate the assumption of technical efficiency, which underlies standard production theory, and would thus preclude finding significant input-to-output relationships.

The theoretical ideal of expenditure analysis envisages a decision maker who knows what objectives he seeks to accomplish and the resources he has at his disposal. He also knows the nature of the process (for example, a production process) by which his objectives are achieved. He reviews the alternative combinations of his resources in terms of some set of criteria and chooses (or allocates resources to) the alternative that leads to the highest level of accomplishment of his goals. Much of the literature on administration and on expenditure analysis deals explicitly or implicitly with the ways decision makers depart from this theoretical ideal. Analysis of expenditure choices in the developing world generally, and in the education sector in particular, departs from the ideal to a considerable degree; not necessarily because of lack of devotion or effort on the part of decision makers but rather due to the characteristics of the educational activities they administer. The approach to expenditure analysis advocated here encounters difficulties at many points. Let us consider several elements in the approach: objective setting, quantifying inputs and outputs, and seeking alternatives.

Objective Setting

Educational objectives are notoriously diffuse and nonoperational. This is due in part to our inability to measure very successfully what it is that education produces. It is also because we expect education to produce many things: cognitive skills, attitudes, values, acculturation, preparation for the world of work, and so on. In the developing world, the expectations for education are very high. On education are pinned the hopes for economic growth, social change, and development of a national identity. Now if analysis of effectiveness involves comparisons between programs in terms of their costs and contributions to objectives, how is one to analyze accomplishment of a bag of objectives that are diverse, often unmeasurable and, if measurable at all, not in the same terms?

There is no truly satisfactory answer to this question, although there are things that can be done. One simply must recognize the limits on the useful domain of economic science. But within that domain, one can attempt to be as clear and explicit about objectives as possible and to develop quantitative measures for those objectives insofar as is feasible and appropriate. And one can, most importantly, suboptimize.

Suboptimization is not desirable in itself. It is merely a necessary device for dealing with complex policy issues that involve multiple objectives. The higher on the hierarchy of decisions one looks at objectives, the more consistency and efficiency it is possible to achieve.

Duplication of effort, programs working at cross-purposes, and wasteful tangential efforts can be spotted more easily from a high-level optimization point of view. And a high level of optimization permits identification of possible complementarities, interactions between programs, and new alternatives for accomplishing the high-level goals.*

But there are limits to high-level optimization, particularly in the education sector. The higher the level of optimization, the larger the number of activities that must be taken into account and the greater their diversity, until the problem becomes conceptually unmanageable. And, the higher the goal, the more general and vague it becomes. One cannot meaningfully measure accomplishment of an educational objective such as "contribute to the quality of life of the person educated." It is possible to break this objective down, however, into several constituent parts: contribute to higher levels of income (which, incidentally, makes possible the achievement of a wide range of other objectives); improve the enjoyment of cultural amenities; foster mobility and a sense of personal efficacy, and so on. Some of these lower-level goals need to be further broken down before one reaches a plane of operational measurability, but the general process is clear. Attempting to clarify an objective and break it down into its constituent parts leads to greater understanding of what ends are desired and increased ability to assess goal accomplishment.

There are problems, to be sure. Some objectives may conflict with others (for example, raising the general level of education tends to stimulate migration out of rural areas, even though many educational programs seek to increase the productivity of rural workers and to stem the flow of rural-to-urban migration). Establishing the trade-off relationships between objectives is possible for an individual but often impossible for a group. And in conflict or bargaining or politically intense situations, clarity of objectives may be a handicap to achieving consensus rather than an aid. In general, however, it helps analysis and the achievement of efficiency if we know what it is that we want to accomplish and have ways of measuring accomplishment. One of the most useful functions of systems analysis, often obscured by concentration on analytical techniques, is its role in clarifying objectives.

---

*These are also the arguments for "coordination" of programs, which is usually viewed as desirable but which encounters strong bureaucratic behavioral opposition. Administrators desire autonomy in their programs (that is, they want to suboptimize in peace) and no one wants to be coordinated.

A final point about objectives relates to the continuous, iterative nature of the planning and analysis process as conceived here. Objectives depend upon the information available and the feasible, available means of achieving them. (This is especially true of lower-level, operational objectives.) This means that as more information becomes available and decision makers become aware of alternative means of achieving desired ends, objectives themselves may change. Awareness of such ends-means interaction is often overlooked in the literature on decision-making (with some notable exceptions), but the interaction is real and important. In developing countries educational objectives tended originally to be conceived in quantitative terms (for example, provide opportunities for all children to obtain a full primary education). As these ends came to be realized more fully, other objectives such as improving the quality or efficiency of education or providing compensatory education for disadvantaged groups became salient. This in turn leads to identification of possible new action programs and changes in strategy and planning. The role of planning as an element in a feedback-based, cybernetic process has been stressed earlier. Such feedback is important for immediate efficiency reasons, but also for its contribution to the evolutionary "learning process" by which national educational strategies are shaped. Clear understanding of what objectives truly are (and how they are changing) is required before there can be feedback on the way the broad program is achieving its purposes.

Quantifying Inputs and Outputs

The ideal decision maker mentioned above knows what his inputs and his outputs are. Here is another point where education differs from the ideal model. Related to the problem of measuring objectives is that of measuring outputs. One can count students easily (quantitative projection planning deals largely with such numbers) but it is far more difficult to measure what they have acquired while passing through the education process.

For a long time observers despaired of being able to measure what education produced, even in partial terms. Most early measurement instruments were group-referenced (that is, they indicated how the individual compared with group norms) rather than criterion-referenced.[34] Group-based measures are difficult to deal with analytically, even if one accepts that they measure meaningful attributes and do so accurately. There are some indications that educational measurement in objective and operational terms may provide an increasingly useful basis for analysis and program improvement.[35] In the United States, Michigan has introduced a statewide program of

42

pupil assessment, based upon a number of instruments measuring operational objectives, which has been used for various policy purposes.[36] Thus improved measurement is feasible.

Even setting aside the developments in the field of measurement, there are readily available ways of finding out what educational programs accomplish. Rate-of-return analysis has long examined the economic effects of adding increments of education and such investigation can be applied in different ways than traditional rate-of-return studies. And if the objective of a given program is to prepare pupils for higher levels of study, it is possible to trace the pupils and learn how graduates of alternative programs (for example, different science curricula) perform at higher levels. Such measurements are not cost free, but neither are the surveys on which manpower and rate-of-return studies are based. And they produce information on performance of programs that is vitally important for analyzing effectiveness and allocating resources to achieve greater efficiency.

If there are some possibilities for measuring outputs, what about measurement of inputs? In most production processes it is easy to measure what goes in. This is not true in education. To take one example, teachers have a significant impact upon educational performance, but our ability to measure teacher quality is severely limited. One can measure the numbers of teachers, their years of education, and their years of experience and these variables do appear to have some explanatory power in production function studies.[37] But there are other factors that also seem to have explanatory power, which have only recently begun to be investigated. H. M. Levin studied data on teachers' verbal and mathematical aptitudes and found a significant relationship between these and indicators of teacher performance.[38] There is growing awareness in the developed world of the need for, and feasibility of, measuring school inputs and outputs.* In the developing world such an awareness needs to be created.

The answers to questions can usually be found, writers on the subject of creativity tell us, once we pass the critical point of asking the right questions. Administrators in developing countries have to become aware of the questions that need to be asked. It is not claiming too much for an economic "way of looking at problems" to say that it helps to focus attention on questions concerning objectives, the

---

*This already-long discussion omits the problem of great gaps in our knowledge of how the education process works, although this is of fundamental importance. Production function studies have encountered difficulties due to the unspecifiability (to date) of a model of the education process. A full discussion would lead far beyond the scope of the present section.

process by which they are achieved, the inputs and outputs of the process, and its productive efficiency. Planning approaches to date have not done so, but this is a key service that a different orientation of economic analysis can provide.

Seeking Alternatives

Planning implies decisions or choices between alternatives. But planning is also often thought to be a matter of determining how to meet needs. Although it may come as a surprise to many, a "needs oriented" concept of planning is inadequate as it is usually applied. The things that differentiate economic choice from needs-oriented planning are several:

1. As discussed above, economic-choice planning asks, "Is that really what you want or need?" (that is, it examines the objective).
2. It asks, "If that is your need, how many ways are there of fulfilling that need?"
3. Given an array of means of meeting the need, economic-choice planners ask, "What is the least costly way of meeting the need?" or, "For a given budget, which alternative makes the greatest contribution to the need?"

Needs-oriented planning, on the other hand, operates on the premise that needs are absolute and usually assumes that provision of more of existing educational services will satisfy the need. To question the "need," for example, for more traditional classroom places when alternative uses of existing space could satisfy growing enrollment, verges on sacrilege. Search for alternatives seems to deny the need.
Economic-choice planning, on the other hand, involves continual questioning: "Why do we want to accomplish this in the first place? Is there a better way of accomplishing it than the present way?" These are particularly important questions in the education sector. Education systems in developing countries tend to be highly centralized and authoritarian in their administrative style. National education programs are usually based on a single syllabus and an approved curriculum. Experimentation is minimal. The only alternatives for comparisons are better and worse degrees of the single form of education. This seriously limits opportunities for analysis and choice.*

---

*Manpower planning is an example of needs-oriented planning, where meeting projected occupational demand is seen as a need and considered absolute.

The difficulties in seeking alternatives in the education sector are of various sorts. In addition to the problem of centralization and homogeneity, there tend to be needs, which, for various reasons—social and political—are given and irreducible. Population grows; enrollment ratios climb; social demand increases. Thus there is a stronger tendency for planning to follow a "needs approach" here than elsewhere. Second, the education sector is affected by an exceptionally high degree of inertia. This is due in part to the attitudes of parents ("If it was good enough for me . . . ."); in part to the political sensitivity (real or imagined) of the subject of education; and in part to the fact that changes in the education sector inevitably involve "retooling" a large stock of human capital: the in-service teaching force. Resistance to change is a universal human trait, tending to be stronger in cases where change involves exertion of individual effort (for instance learning a new curriculum or revising teaching notes), uncertainty ("Will it work?" "Can I teach the new math?" "Will educational television cost me my job?"), and the questioning of various cherished attitudes ("Who says programmed learning can be more effective than an experienced teacher?"). Education is not a new field in any country. Established patterns have existed for long periods. Thus the friction of change is greater than in new fields such as space travel or communications technology. Parents, teachers, and administrators look askance at innovative alternatives. To question existing practices, as an economic analyst or systems analyst characteristically does, is to threaten the practitioners—and to encounter opposition.

Another problem in seeking educational alternatives is that knowledge of the educational process, although growing as a result of current micro-analytical research into the psychology of learning and the effectiveness of education, is still narrowly circumscribed. This lack of knowledge about the implications of change exacerbates the problems of inertia. It is difficult to convince doubters of the value of a change (or of thinking about change) when the benefits of the change are not readily demonstrable. And, also, we simply do not know what all the alternatives are. Can you compress the traditional six-year primary cycle into five, or four? What is the range of applications of programmed approaches? What are the functions that educational television can serve; what can it do better or more cheaply than conventional methods? What effect does a new science curriculum have on development of experimental attitudes and a problem-solving set of mind? The answer to these and other questions is all too often, "We don't know." The more bits of information that are available, the more possibilities for combining information into innovative syntheses (alternatives) there are. The bits of information about the process of education are still sadly limited.

Despite these difficulties, the search for alternatives is an important aspect of the planning process. Alternatives do exist and their consideration and measurement will improve the quality of decisions. In some instances, "natural experiments" such as variations in class size, teacher quality, and other factors within homogenous systems permit some investigation of alternatives. In others planned experiments are required. Lack of hard data on costs, benefits, and external implications makes comparing alternatives difficult. For example, what are the cost and effectiveness implications of introducing a work-study program in vocational schools as opposed to a straight training program? Or, even more perplexing, how do you evaluate two science curriculums, designed to achieve different ends (for example, development of an experimental attitude as opposed to substantive knowledge in a given area) when measurement of either end is extremely difficult and trade-offs between the two are matters of personal preferences.

These problems concerning information on alternatives, and the whole of the preceding section on quantifiability of inputs and outputs, emphasize an important issue that has been passed over very lightly until now: economic analysis of education programs requires information of a sort not generally available. While decisions often cannot wait on lengthy research programs, there is still a need for new information-gathering approaches that produce relevant, performance-related data. The interaction between research and analysis must be much closer than it has been in the past. Chapter 3 will be devoted to this subject.

THE USEFUL DOMAIN OF ECONOMIC
ANALYSIS

It would be possible to expand the discussion of the problems of economic analysis of education questions at great length, as the writer has done elsewhere.[39] Problems concerning the use of analytical models, selection of appropriate criteria for choice, and measurement of externalities, for example, are all significant. But it is not necessary to add more problems to the list in order to perceive that there are some areas in which economic analysis of educational policy decisions has greater utility than in others. It is useful to delineate the domain within which economic analysis and planning is most efficacious so as to avoid excessively high expectations, and to answer the criticisms of some writers who argue that attempts at rational planning are often counter-productive.[40] In large part these criticisms are not of attempts to analyze and achieve efficiency in general, but of attempts to do too much; to apply analysis outside the boundaries of its domain of usefulness.

46

Decisions vary along a number of dimensions and the efficacy of economic analysis is a function of these variations. One dimension that comes immediately to mind is the level of optimization. Economic analysis seems to work better at lower levels of optimization. But if we examine this point, the level of optimization really subsumes several other dimensions. Analysis at higher levels of optimization is difficult because systems boundaries are broader and questions are more complex. Goals are multiple and tend to be vague at higher levels of optimization, data are more difficult to obtain or too highly aggregated to permit detailed analysis, and so on. These dimensions or characteristics of decisions can be listed as follows:

(1) Breadth of the boundaries of the question under consideration;

(2) Complexity of the question;
(3) Clarity and explicitness of goals;
(4) Unity as opposed to multiplicity of goals;
(5) Quantifiability of outputs or of the results of the decision;
(6) Degree of commensurability between outputs;
(7) Degree of certainty or uncertainty of outcomes;
(8) The degree of conflict or bargaining that affects the decision.

Breadth and complexity are fairly straightforward matters to deal with. There are limits to cognitive ability to grasp highly complex situations.[41] This is one basis for Lindblom's arguments against "synoptic" attempts at rational planning: the complexities of over-blown attempts at high-level planning exceed our conceptual abilities to plan.[42] At the other extreme, low-level decisions may be so trivial that there is no need for economic analysis. In the middle range of complexity, analytical tools such as cost-effectiveness permit humans with limited cognitive grasp (aided by the tools and sometimes by computers) to deal with more complex situations than they could on the basis of intuition or rules of thumb. But beyond some undefined point, complexity becomes overwhelming and attempts at analysis may have to involve dangerous oversimplifications. If one attempted to graph the utility of economic analysis with the degree of utility measured on the ordinate and degree of complexity measured to the right on the abscissa, the curve would tend to start low, move upward to a maximum in the middle range of complexity and fall toward (or even cross) the horizontal axis at high levels of complexity.

Clarity of goals tends to be greater at lower levels on the decision hierarchy but depends on other factors as well. The greater the clarity of the ends desired, the more useful economic analysis can be. Purely economic goals can be dealt with most easily. But even noneconomic goals (for example, improving certain achievement

47

scores) can be relatively clear and amenable to analysis. A graph of the direct relationship between goal clarity (measured to the right on the abscissa) and the utility of analysis would show a constantly rising curve sloping upward to the right from the origin.

Multiplicity of goals is frequently the case in educational decisions. The ability of systematic analysis to deal with multiple goals is constrained by a lack of tools. If it is possible to convert second and third goals to money terms this overcomes the problem, but this is rarely the case. Mathematical models that permit analysis of more than one goal are extremely complex. Some attempts have been made to deal with the problem of multiple goals by organizing them into hierarchies, or by optimizing in terms of one goal and then considering the effects on other goals of marginal changes in one direction or another.[43] In general, systematic analysis is useful where a decision involves a single goal (or can be factored into suboptimizing decisions with one goal apiece). A graph of the utility of economic analysis vis-a-vis multiple goals would drop sharply in a stepwise fashion as one moved from one goal to two or more.

Quantifiability has been discussed at length elsewhere. The more clearly one can express the outputs of a program in quantitative terms, the more powerful systematic analysis can be. Quantifiability is not a yes-or-no dimension of decisions because various sorts of proximate outputs, surrogate variables, and proxies can be used to measure outputs and goal accomplishment. The more nearly these quantitative indicators approach direct measurement of the real output, the more useful analysis can be. For example, the rate at which children stay in school beyond the statutory school-leaving age is sometimes considered as a proxy for educational "quality" in a vague sense. Such retention rates are readily measured, but analyses of educational quality based on this indicator would not be strong or highly credible ones.

A point related to both multiplicity of goals and quantifiability of outputs concerns the degree to which multiple outputs can be measured in or converted to the same or commensurable terms. If an educational decision involves, say, both income and employability of graduates, these two outputs can be converted into a single indicator of effectiveness by multiplying the average income of employed workers by the probability of employment. Here analysis can be fully effective. If, in contrast, a decision involves a choice between two alternative science curriculums designed to increase science knowledge and teach an experimental (discovery) method, analyses must be made of each "output" separately and there is no clear means of establishing the trade-offs between the two. The greater the commensurability between outputs, the more useful the tools of analysis.

Decisions often involve uncertain outcomes. The ability of economic analysis to deal with uncertainty has been strengthened by various developments. Using a high discount rate for uncertain economic benefits is one means. Other techniques for analyzing decisions under conditions of uncertainty have come to be called "decision theory," although they apply to only a portion of the decisions faced by administrators.[44] (Schwartz considers two alternative approaches to problems of uncertainty within the framework of cost-effectiveness analysis: sensitivity analysis and contingency planning. These have perhaps greater applicability for uncertainty situations in the education sector than decision theory.)[45] The tools of decision analysis, which are really a branch of applied statistics, involve subjective estimates of the probability of uncertain events (Bayesian "prior probabilities"). Probability estimates are used together with cost and benefit information in order to calculate the "expected value" of one or another outcome of a decision. In a sense, such analytical tools increase in usefulness as greater and greater degrees of uncertainty are involved. This is especially true where there is more than one uncertain variable and intuition alone cannot deal with the decision. But this is only true up to a certain point, beyond which the "reasonableness" of prior probability estimates becomes questionable. A graph of the utility of economic analysis would show utility rising as uncertainty increased, but levelling off and declining at high levels of uncertainty.

A final point concerning the useful domain of economic analysis: in situations where decisions must be made under conditions of conflict or of bargaining, economic analysis, clarification of goals and quantification of outputs may not be desirable. This is one of the arguments advanced by Lindblom and others against overoptimistic uses of planning. Clarity of program aims may be a hindrance to achieving consensus among groups with different interests. As pointed out by Buchannan and Tullock, the costs of making a decision must be taken into account when considering the use of different decision rules.[46] Whitehead considers the role of systems analysis in situations where bargaining between different interest groups exists. He concludes that systems analysis and clear economic arguments may sometimes be used by one party in order to gain advantage in a bargaining situation. It can, however, make the process of bargaining and formation of coalitions more difficult; can be used to "embarrass, stall and confuse."[47] The more nearly the parties to a decision are agreed upon their preferences, the more useful economic analysis can be. If preferences differ, as they do in bargaining and conflict situations, analysis may only sharpen the differences and make compromise and agreement more difficult. Thus analysis becomes less and less useful as greater and greater degrees of conflict and bargaining affect the decision.

These remarks concerning the boundaries of useful applications of economic analysis are intended to support rather than diminish its importance. Criticisms of analytical approaches to decision-making, such as those advanced by Braybrooke and Lindblom and others, seem to be criticisms of applications outside these boundaries. Clarification of when and where analysis can be most useful helps to forestall criticism for the wrong reasons and sharpens the debate between pro-analysis and antianalysis groups. Within the bounded domain of useful applications, economic analysis can make a very great contribution to improved efficiency and effectiveness.

While the points above have tended to be general and abstract, they are highly relevant to analysis in the education sector. Educational expenditure choices must often be made between alternatives for which goals are not clear and outputs are multiple, difficult to measure, and/or incommensurable. This means that economic analysis should be used with care and cannot be used in all circumstances in the education sector. But understanding of the boundaries of usefulness may encourage use of analysis in areas where it has not been applied before.

The boundaries indicated above are not absolute but rather loose and flexible. A two-way dynamic process goes on across them. In one sense decisions may be brought within the useful domain by being broken down into lower-order choices that are less complex, have fewer objectives, and more measurable outputs and so on. In the other direction, the boundaries are being moved outward by developments in the tools of analysis. The development of cost-effectiveness analysis meant that economic analysis could be applied to a far wider range of choices in the education sector than strict benefit-cost analysis could. (Perhaps the past emphasis on the major planning approaches reflects a lack of awareness that these boundaries have shifted.) Development of analytical tools for dealing with uncertainty represents another extension of the useful domain. And finally, improvements in our ability to quantify educational variables (both input and performance variables) increases the applicability and power of analytical tools. Chapter 3 deals with development of better and more complete data for analysis.

The major planning approaches have tended to be used for decisions at a high level of optimization, although the discussion of the useful domain of analysis has indicated that economic analysis tends to be most useful for decisions in the middle range—above the trivial but below the very complex. The principal argument of this chapter has been that economic analysis should be applied throughout its useful domain, not merely for a limited range of decisions. If analytical skills are in short supply, as they are in developing countries, they should be put to work on subjects where they can make the greatest contribution to the quality of decisions.

NOTES

1. C. J. Hitch and R. N. McKean, The Economics of Defense in the Nuclear Age (Cambridge, Mass.: Harvard University Press, 1960), p. 120. Emphasis from the original.

2. R. H. Haveman, "Public Expenditures and Policy Analysis," in R. H. Haveman and J. Margolis, eds., Public Expenditure and Policy Analysis (Chicago: Markham, 1971), pp. 1-18.

3. The literature on benefit-cost analysis is extensive. See A. R. Prest and R. Turvey, "Cost-Benefit Analysis: A Survey," Economic Journal, December, 1965, pp. 683-735. See also: S. B. Chase, Problems in Public Expenditure Analysis (Washington, D.C.: Brookings Institution, 1968); R. Dorfman, Measuring the Benefits of Public Investment (Washington, D.C.: Brookings Institution, 1965); Haveman and Margolis, op. cit., pp. 273-363; and S. Marglin, Public Investment Criteria (Amsterdam: North Holland, 1968).

4. See, for example, T. A. Goldman, ed., Cost-Effectiveness Analysis (New York: Praeger Publishers, 1967).

5. M. Blaug, "Cost-Benefit and Cost-Effectiveness Analysis of Education," Budgeting, Programme Analysis and Cost-Effectiveness in Educational Planning (Paris: OECD, 1969), pp. 173-84.

6. One of the first major works was R. N. McKean, Efficiency in Government through Systems Analysis (New York: Wiley, 1958). A more recent work is Black, Application of Systems Analysis to Government Decisions (New York: Praeger Publishers, 1969).

7. C. J. Hitch and R. N. McKean, op. cit.

8. C. T. Whitehead, Uses and Limitations of Systems Analysis (Santa Monica: RAND Corporation, September, 1967), Report No. P-3683.

9. Black, op. cit.

10. For an annotated bibliography on applications of systems analysis to educational problems and decisions, see OECD, Systems Analysis for Educational Planning: A Selected Annotated Bibliography (Paris: OECD, 1969).

11. Black, op. cit., p. 28.

12. A basic source on program budgeting that considers applications in various U.S. Government programs is D. Novick, ed., Program Budgeting: Program Analysis and the Federal Budget (Washington, D.C.: Government Printing Office, 1964). A series of case studies in applications of program budgeting in various sorts of agencies is found in H. Hinrichs and G. Taylor, Program Budgeting and Benefit-Cost Analysis (Pacific Palisades, Calif.: Goodyear Publishing Company, 1969).

13. For a discussion of developments in the budgetary process, needs for budgetary reform, and arguments pointing toward improved

tools of public expenditure analysis, see A. Smithies, The Budgetary Process in the United States (New York: McGraw-Hill, 1955).

14. For a discussion of the problems of applying PPBS in an education agency, see J. E. Brandl, "Education Program Analysis at HEW," in Haveman and Margolis, op. cit., pp. 549-81.

15. Wildavsky, "Rescuing Policy Analysis from PPBS," in Haveman and Margolis, op. cit., pp. 461-81.

16. H. J. Hartley, Education Planning, Programming, Budgeting: A Systems Approach (Englewood Cliffs, N. J.: Prentice-Hall 1968).

17. This description of the process of economic analysis draws heavily upon the literature on the various analytical tools, particularly on Hitch and McKean, op. cit., pp. 113-20, and on A. Smithies, "Conceptual Framework for the Program Budget," in D. Novick, ed., op. cit., p. 4.

18. See Hitch and McKean, op. cit., pp. 105-31; Prest and Turvey, op. cit.; and Marglin, op. cit.

19. R. McMeekin, "Systems Planning—The Uses and Limitations of a Systems Approach to Education Planning." Mimeographed. Kuala Lumpur, Malaysia: Ministry of Education, Education Planning and Research Division, 1970.

20. See C. E. Lindblom, The Policy-Making Process (Englewood Cliffs, N. J.: Prentice-Hall, 1968); Whitehead, op. cit., pp. 86-115; A. Wildavsky, The Politics of the Budgetary Process (Boston: Little-Brown, 1964), and Haveman and Margolis, op. cit., pp. 367-481.

21. R. Lipsey and K. Lancaster, "The General Theory of the Second Best," Review of Economic Studies 24 (1956): 11-32.

22. Blaug sets out a similar hierarchy in An Introduction to the Economics of Education (London: Allen Lane The Penguin Press, 1970), pp. 127-29.

23. Hitch and McKean, op. cit., p. 162.

24. Ibid., p. 163.

25. A. Smithies remarks on the tendency for programs to become rigid once decisions are made and the need for continuous revision in "Conceptual Framework for the Program Budget," in Novick, op. cit., p. 20.

26. Albert Waterston, Development Planning—Lessons from Experience (Baltimore: Johns Hopkins University Press, 1965), p. 140.

27. R. Dorfman, The Price System (Englewood Cliffs, N. J.: Prentice-Hall, 1964), p. 127.

28. P. H. Coombs and J. Hallak, Managing Educational Costs (New York: Oxford University Press, 1972), pp. 82-83.

29. Ibid., p. xii.

30. "X-efficiency vs. Allocative Efficiency," American Economic Review 56 (1966): 392-415.

31. Ibid., p. 413.

32. Ibid.

33. Ibid., pp. 393-400.

34. P. W. Airasian and G. F. Madaus, "Criterion-Referenced Testing in the Classroom," Measurement in Education (Reports of the National Council in Measurement in Education), 3, no. 4 (May, 1972): 1-8.

35. The Educational Testing Service in Princeton, N. J., has produced numerous papers. See also, for example, H. S. Dyer, "The Concept and Utility of Educational Performance Indicators." Paper read at the Systems and Cybernetics Conference, October, 1967, Boston, Mass. Mimeographed.

36. See "Objectives and Procedures of the Michigan Educational Assessment Program—1970-71," Michigan Department of Education, Assessment Report Number 7, December, 1970; and other reports in this series.

37. See U.S. Department of Health, Education and Welfare, Office of Education, Do Teachers Make a Difference? (Washington, D.C.: Government Printing Office, 1970); a collection of studies examining these and other variables.

38. "A Cost-Effectiveness Analysis of Teacher Selection," Journal of Human Resources 5 no. 1 (Winter, 1970): 24-33.

39. McMeekin, op. cit.

40. C. E. Lindblom, "The Science of Muddling Through," Public Administration Review 19 (1959); and D. A. Braybrooke and Lindblom, A Strategy for Decision (New York: Free Press, 1963).

41. Whitehead, op. cit., pp. 87-94.

42. Braybrooke and Lindblom, op. cit.

43. An approach to handling multiple objectives has been developed with some success by M. L. Manheim and F. L. Hall, Abstract Representation of Goals: A Method for Making Decisions in Complex Problems (Cambridge, Mass.: M.I.T., Department of Civil Engineering, 1965). B. Schwartz treats analysis of multiple educational objectives through sensitivity analysis in an appendix to "Introduction to Program Budgeting and Cost-Effectiveness Analysis in Educational Planning," in Program Budgeting, Program Analysis and Cost-Effectiveness Analysis in Educational Planning (Paris: OECD, 1968), pp. 43-47.

44. Howard Raiffa, Decision Analysis (Reading, Mass.: Addison-Wesley, 1958).

45. B. Schwartz, "Introduction to Programme Budgeting and Cost-Effectiveness Analysis in Educational Planning," in Budgeting, Programme Analysis and Cost-Effectiveness Analysis, op. cit., pp. 34, 51-52.

46. J. M. Buchannan and G. Tullock, The Calculus of Consent (Ann Arbor: University of Michigan Press, 1962), pp. 68-84, 97-116.

47. Whitehead, op. cit., p. 114.

3

DATA FOR ANALYSIS
AND DECISIONS

> To live effectively is to live with
> adequate information.
>   Norbert Wiener[1]

Information does a number of things: (1) it determines our view
of the world; (2) it influences the objectives we establish for ourselves
or for organizations; (3) it shapes the policy questions that administrators ask; (4) it leads to identification of alternative ways of doing
things; and, finally (5) it provides the basis for analysis and choice.
While this is not intended to be a treatise on epistemology, these
multiple aspects of information supply are important. Of particular
importance is the role of information in shaping the questions that
policy makers ask. One of the theses of this study is that much planning, analysis, and data-gathering have been oriented toward wrong
or irrelevant policy questions. This chapter considers the kinds of
data that can be generated which will make it possible to ask—and
answer—more meaningful policy questions.

It is ironic to talk of inadequate educational data when most
educational ministries have descriptive statistics in profusion. Unfortunately, many of the data series available are virtually useless
for purposes of planning change or improving effectiveness. They
do not transcend the realm of data to become information because they
do not provide increments of insight to their users, particularly not
on subjects affecting policy. So, despite vast quantities of numbers,
most ministries cite absence of relevant data as a reason for inadequate planning.

The following sections consider some of the problems that make
it difficult to obtain good data, the theoretical and operational characteristics that policy data should have, and various areas in which research is needed.

Problems of obtaining adequate data are of several sorts. First, data are often incomplete, inaccurate, or both. Second, data tend to be highly aggregated, especially in the case of policy-relevant variables. Third, the data that are available do not measure the variables needed for policy analysis, notably cost and performance variables.

At the most basic level, data for the mere description of education systems have been incomplete and unreliable in many countries. Descriptive data include, for the purposes of this discussion, data on enrollment, wastage, repetition; on the numbers, qualifications and distribution of teachers; and on the costs of existing educational programs. Accurate data on enrollment, wastage, and repetition have been unavailable in some cases and many countries lack data on the numbers and qualifications of teachers, on supply of educational facilities, and especially on the costs of education by level and by major component of cost. Without such data, educational administrators and planners have had to rely on intuition and conjecture when formulating important portions of national education plans.

The efforts of UNESCO and other international agencies to improve educational data in developing countries were greatly needed and have borne fruit.[2] A great deal remains to be done in this area, however; and even if descriptive data were complete, systematic analysis of policy choices and expenditure decisions would require still other sorts of data. An array of descriptive data is a necessary but not a sufficient condition for program evaluation, planning and implementation.

The aggregative nature of most of the data that are available limits their usefulness for analyzing sectoral problems and comparing alternative projects and expenditures. Writers in other fields have remarked on the problems of basing analyses on aggregate data. H. M. Blalock, Jr. has remarked on the problems of aggregation in social science studies other than education.[3] Guy Black describes some problems of aggregated data in carrying out systems analyses in non-defense sectors:

> Not infrequently, the available data are aggregates or averages from many sources, differing in size and in the manner in which they are influenced by the variables in the system model. Yet many of the theories on which models might be based, including most marginal analysis, are directly applicable only to individual decision-making units . . . . However [for reasons of diversity among industries] the marginal technique may not "explain" industry-wide data movements—and model parameters developed to fit industry data are correspondingly irrelevant to any one firm. What are needed are either: (1) models

that are fully valid for aggregates—and theories to support these are particularly difficult—or (2) data for individual firms or decision-making units, data which may be unavailable. This is one reason why systems analysts must so frequently gather fresh data, despite volumes of published aggregative data.[4]

In the education sector, aggregation tends to obscure the regional distribution of educational services, the range of quality between schools, and, importantly, most indications of educational performance.

The third data problem mentioned is that available data do not provide information of the sort needed for policy analysis. Walter Williams draws a useful distinction between two sorts of information: "macronegative" and "micropositive."[5] Macronegative information shows "the dimensions of major problems in broad terms," while micropositive information indicates "what would work in a program."[6] Macronegative information would include indicators of unemployment, differences in educational attainment, excessive dropouts, and so on. Micropositive information, on the other hand, would indicate relationships between programs and their effects: reductions in dropouts resulting from a program, or the combinations of academic, vocational and on-job learning that produce the most successful workers of a given sort.

Most educational data available in developing countries are macronegative. One reason lies in the difficulties of measuring educational performance. Another is that educational data are essentially a byproduct of regular reporting for administrative and regulatory purposes. Enrollment data are gathered because educational financing, assignment of teachers, and other matters depend on them. Data on teachers are gathered for payroll purposes and to assure that pupil/teacher ratios do not exceed established maximums.

It would require a different sort of data to identify possible solutions to educational problems. Different sorts of variables, relating to programs or activities that are within administrators' policy control, are required in order to transcend mere problem identification and begin to indicate positive solutions to problems. Or, where well-known variables are useful, the data must be gathered on a basis that permits specific analysis of program impact.

Data on program performance are essential for cost-effectiveness analysis and other analytical approaches to improving system efficiency. Performance data are indicators of how well the various levels and types of education are achieving their goals. They include data on examination scores, on subsequent performance in later schooling, or on employment and income after leaving school. In a sense, wastage and repetition data provide insights on performance and are borderline cases between descriptive and performance-related data. Data on the rate of implementation of planned construction or other projects are also a form of performance data, although they differ from indicators of educational effectiveness. This discussion is more directly concerned with data on how well programs are operating, what success their graduates have as a result of their experience in the program, and similar questions.

The need to gather information on what programs have accomplished has not been recognized, so "natural" or automatic reporting—as in the case of enrollment data—has not occurred. In addition, there are other reasons why performance data are not reported. First, there are technical difficulties. If objectives are obscure, it is not clear what should be measured. And the "output"-that is, educated graduates—is measured in only the most general, quantitative terms. Where potential indicators of performance such as examination scores are available, poor quality of examinations may create skepticism about what the scores really mean.

Second, there are bureaucratic reasons why educational personnel (including teachers and school administrators) resist performance measures. Performance indicators, if they were available, would impose an unaccustomed burden of accountability. From teacher to school administrator to regional administrator, most persons would rather have full freedom of action than be subjected to scrutiny in terms of performance indicators. Finally, there is a strong conviction on the part of many educators that the real essence of education (whatever it may be) cannot or should not be measured. For all these reasons, information on the results of educational programs is not generally available.

The difficulties of obtaining performance data are real and this paper does not purport to imply that gathering them would be easy. It would, however, be possible to improve greatly upon the present situation. The movement to establish operational objectives and instruments to measure their accomplishment at the micro level has gained considerable momentum in the United States. Efforts to improve and extend measurement have been made by the Educational Testing Service of Princeton, N.J. in both the United States and developing country contexts.[7] Application of economic analysis to the field of education has led researchers to look beyond the school's walls to future employment and earnings for measures of effectiveness, and the same principle can be applied to measurement of even nonmonetary objectives (for example, future performance of graduates of specific programs in later schooling). Finally, some proximate indicators of program performance can be developed, especially in the area of program implementation.

Practical problems create barriers to even the most basic data gathering, and these problems vary from country to country. In some countries, different scheduling of the school year in different regions, due to climatic conditions or harvest seasons, greatly complicates the problem of providing basic enrollment data on a timely basis. Double-session employment of teachers makes it difficult to measure the existing stock of teachers. Universities with large part-time enrollment and part-time faculties find it hard to measure either enrollment or staff on a full-time equivalent basis. Data on private education are usually hard to obtain. There are technical means to overcome many of these problems, but a full discussion is outside the scope of this study. Here we focus upon the criteria for a data system that will produce micropositive information on ways to improve the education system.

THE NATURE OF POLICY-RELEVANT DATA

The discussion below is divided into two categories: general criteria and operational characteristics of data systems. The line between the two categories is sometimes blurred but the distinction is useful. In the more general or theoretical realm, the findings of information systems studies indicate that data for use by management should be: oriented toward the user, economical to gather, flexible, relevant, simple, timely, complete, accurate, and easy to recall from "storage."[8] It should be clear from reading this list that some of these criteria compete with others. No set of data can be perfect, and administrators and planners must trade off improvements in one dimension against sacrifices in another. For example, gains in completeness may involve losses in timeliness. Increased flexibility of data for multiple analytical purposes may involve increases in cost, as would greater speed, accuracy or completeness. Only the administrators who will use the data can decide how the trade-offs are to be made.

General Criteria for Data

Data should be User-Related. Analysts attempting to utilize data frequently find that they are not compiled in a way that permits meaningful analysis. In budget data, to cite an important example, expenditures are usually categorized by item (for example, "textbook expenditures," or "vehicle costs," or "chalk") rather than by function, by level of education, or by major component of expenditure. One of the first problems encountered in implementing a program budgeting system is how to categorize expenditure data in a way that will permit meaningful analysis of expenditures. Unfortunately, any form of categorization has shortcomings, as program budgeting practitioners have learned. It is possible, however, to make major improvements in the categorization of expenditure and other data over the usual patterns found in developing countries. The basic step of calculating unit costs (for example, teaching costs per student, or administrative cost per student or per school) often provides great improvements in the information content or "insight value" of cost data. Efforts to organize data in a form that will be of greatest use to administrators are often hampered because the administrators do not know what questions they want to ask or to what uses the data might be put. Time and effort spent in clarifying these questions at an early stage make it possible to avoid costly and often futile data-gathering activities later on. Achieving user-relatedness is a two-way process in which administrators as much as planners and statisticians need to give careful consideration of their information needs. These points will arise again in the discussion of operational characteristics of data.

Data Gathering Should be Economical. Information is costly. "Automatically reported" data may be less expensive to gather than data that require special efforts, but even automatically reported data involve costs of compilation, transmission, tabulation, storage, and access. The costs of handling data, should be reduced where possible. This has often been done by omitting detail, but the result may be a loss of important information. One of the most effective cost-saving methods is to determine what variables are needed for measurement and analysis before major new information systems are established. Like the effort to determine users' needs, time spent in specifying variables can lead to major savings later. For example, most education systems disaggregate all pupil data by sex (partly because it is a readily observable trait). While data on enrollment by sex may be useful for some purposes, they compound the costs and work involved in gathering and tabulating all pupil data and the need for data by sex should be carefully examined. If less expensive alternative sources of the information needed can be found, these alternatives should be investigated (for example, use of sampling techniques, or disaggregation by sex at only specified levels).

Special purpose studies are the most expensive source of information, yet sometimes they are the most cost-effective means of obtaining the information needed. If regular reporting sources do not produce data on key variables, and if the value of the information is great enough to justify gathering it, then special purpose surveys or samples are indicated. If they are well designed, these can produce information at reasonable cost. Capability to design sample surveys, however, has usually been scarce in ministries of education.

A Data System Should be Flexible. This can have two meanings. In one sense, it may mean that some series can be added or dropped on a flexible basis, which may be desirable. The second meaning of flexibility is more important. Data should be gathered and compiled in such a way that they can be used for a number of different purposes. This is not a simple or inexpensive task. The principal means by which analytical flexibility is accomplished is by maintaining a fairly high degree of disaggregation and specificity. The discussion of the operational characteristics of data considers the importance of organizing data in a way that permits cross-tabulation and multivariate analysis. In the present context, it is sufficient to say that, if a study is conducted at some trouble and expense (for example, a survey of teacher qualifications), it should be possible to relate the data from this study to other studies (for example, studies of pupil performance or of educational costs).

Data Gathering Should be Simple. Compilation of data, whether on a regular or a special basis, can impose such burdens or costs on the educational system that the benefits in terms of information gained are not worth the effort required to gather the data. This trade-off between benefits and costs of data gathering should be borne in mind in planning any regular series or special study.

Data Should be Available on a Timely Basis. Obviously, if information is needed for an annual budgeting exercise, it must be available at a certain time or its value is largely lost. In other cases, rapid compilation and presentation of data are less critical but still important. Data made available long after the period in which they are gathered may become obsolete before they ever reach the analyst or decision maker. Especially in the evaluation of new or experimental programs, rapid feedback of information is of great importance. Timeliness is traded off most directly against completeness, degree of detail, and to some extent, accuracy. Use of sampling techniques rather than full surveys, elimination of some detail and use of estimates rather than definitive measurements (for example, of costs) all permit greater speed of data gathering. Problems of sampling error, loss of important information through omitting detail, and possible inconsistencies between estimated and directly-measured data impose limits on the extent to which these methods can be used. The administrator must decide how to assess the trade-offs. In some cases it is preferable for him to have imperfect data when he needs it rather than better data when it is too late.

Data Should be Complete. All too frequently, data are gathered on a regular basis for only a portion of the education system. If educational activities are carried on in a number of ministries (for example,

60

if vocational training is provided by a wide array of agencies), or if the private sector plays a significant role, compilation of data on only a part of the broad educational system may lead to erroneous policy conclusions. In at least one country, overlooking the role of private teacher training colleges led to serious overinvestment in public teacher training facilities. While some uses of data may not require completeness, comprehensive data should be available in order to provide a full perspective on major aspects of the education system. And if partial data are utilized, this fact should be made clear to the user.

Data Should be Accurate. The issue of accuracy is not as black and white as it might seem. As noted above, it is sometimes useful to utilize estimates rather than direct measurements for the sake of greater speed or economy. One first step to improve accuracy and reliability is to identify and guard against possible biases in reporting. If grants or teacher assignments are based upon enrollment, a strong incentive exists to inflate enrollment figures. Attendance may likewise be over reported because low attendance rates may reflect badly upon teachers and administrators. In addition to checking for possible biases, it is desirable to check for errors of interpretation or mere clerical errors. Spot verifications of accuracy are useful, as are internal checks on consistency (for example, separate series that should add to the same total, or tables that permit cross-checking of clerical accuracy). It takes a sophisticated data user to realize that accuracy is a relative rather than an absolute matter, and to be satisfied with a reasonable degree of reliability rather than perfection.

Data Should be Accessible. Electronic data processing and improved storage and retrieval offer major improvements in the ease with which data can be marshalled for analysis. Particularly in cases where disaggregation leads to large quantities of detailed data, machine processing may make it possible to overcome major barriers imposed by physical limitations on data handling. Establishment of large data banks should be undertaken with care, however. This may be a futile and costly exercise unless the information system is carefully planned to permit access to the data. Once again, it is of fundamental importance to know the uses to which the data will be put at the time the information system is designed.

Operational Characteristics of Data

Beyond the general criteria discussed above, there are a few characteristics that a data set should have in order to be useful for policy analysis. The most important of these are policy-relevance, specificity to the unit of observation, longitudinality (in some cases), and relation to educational performance and costs. Not all of these characteristics will be present in a single data series, but the full set of data available to policy makers should include elements with all of these characteristics.

Data Should be Policy Relevant. As noted above, data should be gathered with the needs of their ultimate users in mind. A further elaboration of this point is that data should relate to variables over which decision makers have some degree of policy control. To give, an example, a study of the relationship between wastage and family income, by region, may reveal strong correlations between the two. Since educational policy makers have no control over family income, however, the results of such a study may offer little more information than what intuition would provide, and no guidance for policy. Studies incorporating variables relating to the burden of school fees, private costs of education (for example, for clothing, books, and supplies) and the levels of subsidy that would enable poor children to continue schooling, produce information that is a useful guide to action. Design of such studies is a matter of asking the right questions. General studies may be necessary in order to discover and refine the policy questions to be asked, but the ultimate value of information for planning and administration lies in the guidance it provides for action.

Data Should Generally be Disaggregated and Specific to the Relevant Unit of Observation. When data are aggregated, information is lost. Among the first losses are insights into program performance and effectiveness. The unit of observation is some studies may be the school or the class, but even this degree of aggregation may obscure what happens to individual pupils. What is sought is relationships between "treatment" variables (teachers, texts, or experimental programs) and their impact on performance. Information on such relationships requires micro-analysis of educational functions.

It should be possible to relate one variable to another at the level of observation, either in simple cross-tabulations or in multivariate analyses. Separate studies of individual variables may be an improvement over the total absence of some data in the past. But the scope, flexibility and power of data are greatly enhanced if it is possible to relate several variables to each other. This means that considerable detail must be maintained, which involves costs. The role of machine processing of data is important here. The most important factor, however, is a clear understanding at the outset of the analytical uses to which data will be put.

Data Sets Should Include Information on Educational Performance.
The data available influence the policy questions that administrators
ask. Questions on how well the education system is working, or on
what variables influence its success tend to be avoided because no
data are available on which to base answers. The vicious circle of
wrong or irrelevant policy questions and inadequate data on performance can be broken through well-designed research. This need has
not been recognized or understood, even in developed countries, until
recently. Data can play an important role in improving educational
effectiveness, simply by casting light on what constitutes effectiveness.

Among the most powerful tools for measuring educational performance are longitudinal studies, tracing graduates of various levels
or types of education through higher levels of education or in work
experience. Remarking on some shortcomings of past research on
U.S. educational programs, Alice Rivlin asks: "What would it take
to do a better job?" Her answer is that, assuming a fairly stable
relationship between inputs and outputs and variations between natural
experiments, three things are needed for more meaningful research:

> (1) a longitudinal data system for keeping track of individ-
> ual children as they move through school and for record-
> ing changes in their performance; (2) detailed program
> information and resource information at the level of the
> individual child . . . ; (3) information on the child's own
> family background to be taken into account in assessing
> the effects of the school on the child.[9]

Blalock notes that:

> If we know time sequences as well as correlations, we
> are in a better position to choose among alternative ex-
> planations. This fact has important implications for re-
> search design, since it implies that, whenever possible,
> we should collect data at more than one point in time.[10]

Since direct measurement of the impact of an educational program is often difficult, program effects may be measured best in
terms of later experiences of graduates. Cross-section studies of
differences in educational treatment (whether in "natural" or experimental situations) cannot provide as much information as longitudinal
studies. Single evaluations of programs after their completion often
fail to provide information on the causes of success or nonsuccess.
In other fields (for example, agriculture or rural development) the
importance of longitudinal panel studies has long been recognized.
Data with significant explanatory power can best be obtained by

tracing individuals as they are exposed to programs. At the very least, "before and after" measurements should be made, but even this has not been fully acknowledged in the education sector.

Data on Costs are Necessary. The need to gather data on costs has been almost as much overlooked as the need for performance data. As noted by Coombs and Hallak, "Educational systems and institutions, even in the most highly industrialized countries, have not been very 'cost conscious.'"[11] Cost data are important for the most basic tasks of management, planning, and control of educational organizations, from the level of the school to the level of national systems. Even the most straightforward projections of budgetary requirements are impaired by the absence of sound, reliable cost information. But beyond descriptive measurement and control uses, cost data have an extremely important analytical role. They are an essential ingredient of cost-effectiveness analysis. If performance data are the lever of analysis, cost data are the fulcrum. Together they provide the basis for informed choices on how to achieve the greatest possible improvements in an education system with the resources available.

Data Gathering Should be Cost-Effective. Just as the tools of cost-effectiveness analysis should be applied to educational programs, they should similarly guide the development of a data system. If the costs of a study are too great, then it should not be performed. Or, more desirably, ways should be found to obtain the same information at lower cost. One means of reducing data-gathering costs is through sample studies.

The reliability of sample studies (given certain conditions) is not generally understood by non statisticians. Few administrators of developing educational systems recognize that a well-designed sample survey can produce policy information that is virtually as accurate as a one-hundred percent census; and that sampling can improve the manageability of data by avoiding data glut, reducing costs, and increasing speed of analysis. The net result is that it is often possible to obtain useful policy information more effectively through sampling than through full surveys. Proper design of the sampling technique with regard to the sample frame, randomization, stratification if desired, and so on, are necessary and can make the difference between meaningful information and relatively useless data.

Since special studies may be needed in order to obtain policy data on performance, costs, and so on, and since the costs of ad hoc data gathering are high, sampling offers a means to reduce the costs and other burdens of such studies. Many of the criteria and characteristics of data discussed above involve high costs and the need to trade off one desirable factor against another is great. Sample studies act to alleviate some constraints, so that it is possible to obtain more of the desired ends within the research and information budget available. Particularly in the area of longitudinal performance studies and investigation of costs, sampling techniques can make it feasible to conduct policy research that has rarely been done before in developing countries due to cost, time, or manpower constraints.

The level of competence in data management and analysis in developing countries is generally low. Considerable competence is needed in order to design information systems efficiently, minimize data gathering costs, provide the information policy makers need, investigate performance and costs on the basis of sound analytical techniques, employ sampling methods, and other subjects discussed above. This is an area in which technical assistance and training efforts of international agencies can make a highly significant contribution to improving the quality of information. This in turn can lead to major improvements in educational effectiveness.

NEEDS FOR FURTHER RESEARCH

It is customary to list topics for further research in a concluding chapter, but since the preceding sections have dealt with the characteristics of data and research needed for educational planning and administration, it seems appropriate to consider some specific research needs here. The brief list below is certainly not definitive. Special problems and characteristics of each national educational system undoubtedly require different sorts of data and specific studies for policy purposes. The brief listing of research topics is intended to indicate some of the general needs for research that are rarely met in developing countries.

1. In the area of descriptive data, there is a need for simple, deterministic models of enrollment flows through the education system, with related submodels that show teacher requirements (net increase plus attrition) and capital and recurrent costs by level of education. Flow models make it possible to project enrollment, teacher requirements and costs implied by alternative policies or varying assumptions.

2. Sample studies of schools by level of education can provide information on the following variables:

(a) enrollment, promotion rates, and retention rates;
(b) "environmental characteristics" such as double or single sessions, urban or rural location, and socio-economic level of the community;

(c) supply and condition of physical facilities such as buildings, laboratories, and libraries;

(d) teacher supplies and qualifications: number, specialization, education, years' experience, turnover rates;

(e) sources of funds, including: central government grants and subventions, local public funds, tuition and fees, other sources of income, and savings on hand, if any;

(f) actual expenditures by category: teaching and administrative salaries, occupancy costs, instructional materials and equipment, and other categories of expenditure;

(g) qualitative assessment of schools in terms of quality of facilities (for example, library quality and accessibility), attitudes, variables related to administration, "academic climate," and so on;

(h) indicators of performance wherever possible, including promotion and retention rates, average scores on national achievement tests when available, and other performance-related variables.

Such studies should permit cross tabulation of different subsets of variables, which would permit a variety of special studies. For example, studies of economies of scale, of costs by category, of adequacy of school revenues, of regional differences in various senses, and of the distribution of qualified teachers would be possible. If performance data were available, studies of relationships between educational inputs and performance would provide the kind of micropositive data discussed above. If sample studies were updated periodically, there would be a continuing data base for a wide array of basic policy analyses. Few developing countries if any possess such a data base.

3. Small sample studies of the causes of retention and wastage, with emphasis on investigation of means by which educational policies could improve the existing situation, would be very useful.

4. Investigation of the capital costs of school buildings by type and by major components of capital cost would make capital cost projections more reliable. Such studies could also investigate school building maintenance and repair needs. Investigations of ways to reduce capital costs could be undertaken in connection with descriptive studies.

5. Detailed investigations of vocational education are generally needed. In addition to the variables listed in item 2 above, other variables specific to vocational schools should be investigated, including:

(a) the quality and relevance of vocational course materials;

(b) adequacy of facilities for practical instruction (shop equipment, its maintenance and reliability, and so on);

(c) special costs of vocational education including, for example, costs of expendable materials;

(d) balance between in-class and practical (that is workshop) time;

(e) background characteristics of students, including prior academic records, reasons for attending vocational school, occupational orientation and preferences, awareness of employment opportunities and of placement assistance available, and attitudes toward vocational education and future work;

(f) attitudes of administrators toward vocational education, their perceptions of the goals of vocational education, efforts to assure pupil placement, principal problems they encounter, and possible related subjects.

6. Sample-based longitudinal studies of vocational graduates are greatly needed. (Such a study is discussed in Chapter 5.) Studies should investigate employment rates, starting salaries, promotion rates, relevance of education to the jobs obtained, individual background (see item 5 (e) above) including vocational school attended, trade course taken, grades obtained, and similar variables. Attitude studies including graduates' assessments of their education and its usefulness to them, and employers assessments of vocational graduates' performance in comparison with other workers, can provide additional information that can be fed back into the vocational school program.

7. There is also a need for sample-based longitudinal studies of the experience of school leavers from various levels and kinds of schools, especially at the middle and upper secondary levels. Such studies could examine the experience of those who graduated as well as those who dropped out. Information could be collected on graduates who continued their education as well as those who sought work. In the former category, information is needed on academic performance of graduates including later academic career, grades, and teachers' assessments. If such information is gathered for graduates of different kinds of education (for example, science vs. arts graduates or graduates from schools experimenting with new curriculums or course materials) it provides insight into the educational effectiveness of various educational alternatives. For graduates who sought work, sample studies could examine their employment rates and starting salaries. Again, comparison of the experience of graduates of alternative kinds of education (for example, comprehensive schools vs. purely academic schools) would provide a basis for evaluating alternatives.

8. There is a need for studies of school administration that can measure the efficiency of school management (for example, utilization of staff and facilities capacity) and the role of administrators in

improving school effectiveness, preparing graduates for higher levels of education or, in the case of vocational or comprehensive schools, for the world of work. The characteristics of effective school managers should be investigated to provide information for future selection processes.

9. There is a general need for research in the area of measurement of educational performance. While considerable work on educational measurement is carried out in developed countries, the instruments used have to be adapted to developing country situations. In addition, it is entirely possible for investigators in developing countries to explore performance measures based not on testing but on longitudinal studies of graduates' later success in academic or economic terms.

Possibilities for combining some of these research areas are obvious. For example studies of administration could be included with descriptive studies of educational services (item 2 above). Or studies indicating graduates' performance could be related to educational quality variables for the schools attended to identify possible causal relationships. Combinations of studies would permit evaluation of alternative kinds of education and testing of various hypotheses. The resulting information would have far greater insight value for decision makers than the usual array of descriptive data.

While evaluation of existing educational programs should be carried on continuously, special research on experimental programs is also inportant. Many highly centralized educational systems in developing countries offer few opportunities for comparing alternatives because few differences exist between schools. Even in monolithic educational systems, it is sometimes possible to identify "natural" experimental situations (for example, groups of schools that happen to have marked differences in teacher quality, and so on). Here it is of great importance to plan the research design at the outset rather than gather data first to see what it reveals. Efforts should be made to develop experimental alternatives designed to improve educational effectiveness. Some experimentation has been done in developing countries but this has often been poorly conceived from a research standpoint and has produced little sound information. Once again, the research design for evaluating educational experiments must be carefully planned. This is far from easy, as evaluators of experiments in the United States have learned. But it is not impossible, and the information produced can effect major changes in the quality and cost of education.

Given the major needs and limited capabilities for research, the planning and scheduling of research should be based on a system of priorities. Particular problem areas, educational levels that will be subject to major policy decisions, or programs that absorb a large portion of educational resources should receive the highest priority for investigation.

The following chapters present a case study based upon an unusual combination of data sources. These will hopefully illustrate in greater detail some of the kinds of research recommended here, as well as some of the policy and planning uses to which the resulting data can be put.

NOTES

1. Norbert Weiner, The Human Use of Human Beings, rev. ed. (New York: Doubleday, 1954), p. 18.

2. J. D. Chesswas, Methodologies for Educational Planning for Developing Countries (Paris: UNESCO/HEP, 1969), is an example.

3. H. M. Blalock, Jr., An Introduction to Social Research (Englewood Cliffs, N.J.: Prentice-Hall, 1970), pp. 76-77.

4. G. Black, Application of Systems Analysis to Government Decisions (New York: Praeger Publishers, 1969), pp. 122-23.

5. W. Williams, Social Policy Research and Analysis: The Experience in the Federal Social Agencies (New York: Elsevier, 1971), p. 7.

6. Ibid.

7. See H. S. Dyer, "The Concept and Utility of Educational Performance Indicators," Paper read at the 1967 Systems Science and Cybernetics Conference, October 1967, at Boston; Mass. Mimeographed.

8. I. B. Turksen and A. G. Holzman, "Information Design for Educational Management," Socio-Economic Planning Sciences 6 (February, 1972): pp. 1-20.

9. A. Rivlin, Systematic Thinking for Social Action (Washington, D.C.: Brookings Institution, 1971), pp. 76-77.

10. Blalock, op. cit., p. 72.

11. P. H. Coombs and J. Hallak, Managing Educational Costs (New York: Oxford University Press, 1972), pp. 82-83.

4

A CASE STUDY OF
UPPER SECONDARY
EDUCATION POLICY
IN MALAYSIA

One would like to present a case study that: (1) demonstrated clearly the uses of economic analysis advocated in earlier chapters; (2) incorporated analyses that led to clear and unambiguous conclusions; and (3) described a policy choice based upon the analysis. If there were many such examples, however, the arguments of the preceding chapters would have been unnecessary. What is offered in this chapter instead is an example based upon a real, complex policy question that arose in Malaysia around 1970. At issue was what portion of candidates should be permitted to proceed from the lower secondary to the upper secondary level—that is, how rapidly the upper secondary level should be permitted to expand in relation to other levels. This was a fairly high-level question, theoretically amenable to analysis in terms of manpower needs or relative rates of return. But as we shall see, the question broke down into several lower-level, subordinate questions and side issues, and the information provided by manpower and rate-of-return studies was not sufficient to guide the choice of an access rate. Availability of an unusual body of policy information makes it possible to illustrate various kinds of suboptimizing analyses.

The case and the policy questions are structured in a more clear and choice-oriented way than the rather casual manner in which the issues arose in real life. What is presented is not a report of how analyses and choices were actually made but rather an indication of how the issues might have been treated, if Malaysian policy makers and their then-advisor had enjoyed the benefits of hindsight and more time for reflection. The conclusions that emerge are suggestive, not definitive. As is usually the case with policy analysis, new questions are raised in the course of answering the old ones. The need for still more data is clear. The case includes a discussion of access to upper secondary education and related issues in this chapter, plus a separate examination of the vocational education alternative in Chapter 5. Its objectives are as follows:

1. To demonstrate the feasibility of gathering policy-relevant data of the sort described in Chapter 3;
2. To illustrate the way that manpower and rate-of-return analyses provide partial information but are not, either alone or in combination, sufficient tools to illuminate many important policy questions;
3. To indicate the way that high-level policy issues such as the access question break down into lower-level questions amenable to suboptimizing analyses.
4. To demonstrate ways in which available analytical tools and policy-relevant data can provide information on the full hierarchy of policy choices and indicate possible improvements in the internal effectiveness of a portion of a developing education system.

EXPANSION OF MALAYSIAN UPPER SECONDARY EDUCATION

The background of the upper secondary policy issue lay in earlier decisions that had far-reaching implications. In the mid-nineteen sixties, the Malaysian Secondary School Entrance Examination (or the "eleven-plus" exam) was eliminated and an automatic promotion scheme was adopted for the first nine years of schooling.* These decisions had the effect of opening access to lower secondary education (Forms I through III) to greatly increased numbers of students. As one result, the number of students completing the lower secondary cycle and seeking admission to upper secondary (Forms IV and V) rose from 53,000 in 1965 to 96,000 in 1970. Entry to Form IV continued to be limited by the Lower Certificate of Education examination (LCE in the English language medium; SRP in Malay medium).

While the number of students promoted to Form IV also increased (from 22,000 in 1965 to 43,000 in 1970), a policy question arose regarding the continued expansion of the upper secondary level. Short run limitations of teachers and classroom places made it necessary to limit access to Form IV severely when the wave of

----

*Appendix A presents a brief description of the Malaysian education system that provides a factual background and context for the discussions in this chapter. All references to "Malaysia" mean West Malaysia, and exclude from consideration the Borneo states, which have somewhat different education systems.

increased lower secondary enrollment reached Form IV. The "promotion pass" rate fell from its previous level of over 60 percent of all candidates in 1965-66 to less than 50 percent in 1969-70. The absolute numbers of pupils entering upper secondary increased, but the proportion of candidates who were admitted fell. This led to substantial popular pressure for more access and forced the issue to the attention of policy makers. Although this is the sort of situation where manpower and rate-of-return analysis should be able to provide guidance, their findings were in conflict, as we shall see later.

The access question had various levels and ramifications. Important among these was the question of interracial equity. In view of Malaysia's political situation in 1969-70, the policy question, "How much access should be permitted?" could not be isolated from the question, "Who would benefit from increased access?" A portion of this chapter deals with the ways in which data and analysis can cast light upon various aspects of the equity question.

The high-level question of how much upper secondary enrollment should be allowed to grow had still other internal or lower-level aspects. The arguments for limiting access were based on the assumptions that graduates of the academic upper secondary stream were prepared only for middle-level "white collar" employment and that suitable employment opportunities could not be found for increased numbers.* Thus there would be overproduction of academic upper secondary graduates. But if the nature of upper secondary education could be changed so as to prepare graduates for other sorts of employment, then the overproduction problem would be eliminated by definition. This obviously affected the access question.

There were several alternative means of changing the nature of the upper secondary level. One apparent solution would have been to increase the vocational stream as a proportion of total upper secondary enrollment. This was strongly advocated by a number of observers, including representatives of the World Bank. For a number of reasons, however, this was neither as easy nor as desirable as it appeared. Chapter 5 treats the choice between academic and vocational education in detail and this alternative will not be considered in the present chapter.† Another approach would have been to shift

---

*Students completing Form V and entering the labor market will be referred to as "graduates" for convenience, although the group included both those who passed the Malaysian Certificate of Education (MCE) examination (but failed to gain access to Form VI) and those who did not "graduate" with a passing grade.

†Such separation of the vocational education issue from the main access question is not only convenient but also corresponds to

the balance of academic enrollment from the arts stream to the science stream, on the assumption that science graduates were better equipped to find blue-collar and technical employment and therefore would not be in surplus. A third alternative would have been adoption of a comprehensive education model for the upper secondary level.* If all graduates were given some exposure to prevocational courses in addition to academic courses, the argument went, they would be better prepared to enter a wider range of occupations. The problem of overproduction of purely academic graduates would therefore be resolved. These alternatives were all considered at the time in Malaysia, although not in an explicit sense as alternatives nor in direct relation to the access question.

After reviewing the quantitative implications of different access rates, the findings of manpower and rate-of-return studies and the equity implications of the access policy, this chapter will examine these alternatives to see what information economic analysis could provide for policy makers. The access question and related policy issues are more complex than a single, high-level choice between different amounts of enrollment in different levels. There is an hierarchy of decisions ranging from resource allocations at the top, through social and political factors, to the internal content of upper secondary education and comparison of vocational and other alternatives. It is hoped to show how economic analysis (including different applications of manpower and rate-of-return analysis) can be oriented to provide information on the full range of policy choices.

An unusual array of data relating to upper secondary education became available before or around the time that the access policy was under consideration. These data, which exhibit some of the operational characteristics discussed in Chapter 3, will be discussed briefly before proceeding further. The case study then examines:

(1) The quantitative implications of increasing access, including the budgetary effects of choosing different access rates;

(2) The findings of manpower and rate-of-return studies and the information they provide regarding access policy;

---

the way vocational education was considered separately in Malaysia at the time.

*The comprehensive education concept had been adopted at the lower secondary level some years before, with the inclusion of four vocational "electives" intended to expose all students to industrial arts, agriculture, home science, or commercial courses. The alternative was therefore phrased in terms of "extending comprehensive education upward through Form V."

(3) The relationships between access rates and interracial equity, an important issue in Malaysia at the time; and

(4) The several policy alternatives that might have been considered in connection with the access question.

Data for Analysis of Upper Secondary Education

Policy makers pondering what proportion of candidates to admit to Form IV had data at their disposal that permitted more complete and diverse analyses of the policy question than is usually possible in developing countries. The data set was not completely satisfactory by any means, but it offered several opportunities for policy investigations that illustrate some of the points raised in earlier chapters. Even though not all the opportunities for analysis were taken at the time, the case (including Chapter 5) still offers an instructive example of what could be done with policy-relevant information.

A number of special studies had been carried out by government agencies or private individuals and a considerable body of data was available. In 1967 a Socio-Economic Survey of West Malaysia was conducted by the Department of Statistics.[1] This large sample survey of households produced data on education, occupation, income, and employment that made an analysis of rates of return to education possible. Such an analysis was carried out by O. D. Hoerr, an advisor to the Economic Planning Unit in the prime minister's department.[2] The Department of Labor and Department of Statistics conducted a manpower survey of selected economic sectors (with emphasis on public sector employment) in 1965.[3] This study had a number of limitations but did provide some broad assessment of the manpower situation. Both these studies were somewhat out of date by the time the issues concerning upper secondary education arose, but they and several subsequent analyses based upon them provided useful background information on the relative rates of return to differing levels of education and on the situation with regard to manpower supply and utilization.

Three other special studies produced primary data that were not available from regular reporting sources. In 1970 and 1971, a sample survey of Malaysian upper secondary schools was conducted by Harold S. Beebout. The study was sponsored by the Education Planning and Research Division (EPRD) of the Ministry of Education. The writer, then Ford Foundation advisor to the EPRD, participated in the design of the survey. Dr. Beebout has kindly made the basic data available for use in the present study. The sample survey gathered a wide array of data on the educational inputs provided by the schools (teacher qualifications, facilities, and so on), the costs

of each school by category, and a longitudinal measure of pupil performance based on individual entering and leaving scores on national
examinations. A preliminary report was prepared in 1971, presenting
some of the basic data from the survey.[4] Subsequent analysis of the
"production surface" for upper secondary education was completed
in 1972.[5] Appendix B describes this survey and its methodology in
greater detail.

A special study of the capital costs and utilization of secondary
school buildings was conducted by experts from the UNESCO-sponsored
Asian Regional Institute for School Building Research in Colombo
Ceylon.[6] General information on school building size, characteristics
and utilization was gathered for the country as a whole. On the basis
of this information a representative sample school was chosen and
its actual costs analyzed in detail. While the methodology of selecting
a single sample school can be questioned on reliability grounds, this
approach provides an interesting example of low-cost, mission-
oriented research that produces data not otherwise available.

A longitudinal survey of graduates of upper secondary vocational
schools in West Malaysia was performed by I. Lourdesamy in 1970-71.[7]
This study gathered data on employment rates and income of vocational
graduates, as well as other variables, that provide insight into the
effectiveness of vocational education as an alternative to academic
upper secondary education.

While each of the studies cited above has limitations and shortcomings, together they provide an unusual array of data for policy
analysis. The last three in particular exhibit many of the desired
characteristics of policy-relevant data discussed in Chapter 3: disaggregation and analysis at the level of the individual school or pupil,
longitudinality, detailed examination of costs in relation to other
variables, and investigation of performance. Data from these studies
will be used in the rest of this chapter in analyzing some of the policy
questions affecting upper secondary education.

QUANTITATIVE IMPACT OF INCREASED ACCESS
TO UPPER SECONDARY

As noted, the automatic promotion policy and elimination of the
qualifying examination for entrance to the secondary level produced
a wave of increased enrollment that moved upward in successive
years until it reached the upper secondary level. Table 4.1 shows
enrollment in the sixth grade plus lower and upper secondary level
enrollment for the period 1963 through 1970. Note the major jump
in Form I enrollment in 1965 and the later impact of this increase.

TABLE 4.1

Total Enrollment in Grade 6 and Secondary Forms I
through V, 1963–70

	1963	1964	1965	1966	1967	1968	1969	1970
Grade 6	148,819	160,792	161,817	171,819	179,604	192,409	188,339	200,665
Form I	45,798	44,286	84,925	105,197	112,598	117,334	119,575	128,707
Form II	35,680	46,286	51,271	82,710	99,863	103,860	107,549	107,348
Form III	31,509	36,552	52,756	50,568	82,922	92,263	92,263	95,943
Form IV	12,715	17,728	22,242	31,939	33,590	42,585	46,023	43,089
Form V	11,968	12,864	18,513	23,537	32,522	34,773	42,989	46,614

Note: The data are for "Assisted Schools," which account for virtually 100 percent of enrollment at the primary level and a very high percentage of enrollment at the secondary level. Enrollments for all media are combined. Enrollment in the "remove" or language transition year is omitted.

Source: Educational Statistics of Malaysia, 1938 to 1967, Education Planning and Research Division (Kuala Lumpur: Dewan Bahasa dan Pustaka, 1967; and data prepared by the EPRD).

The quantitative projection approach to planning would address the access question by projecting the effects of the wave of increased enrollment and estimating the pupil places, teachers, and so on needed to provide for the projected enrollment. The social demand approach might interpret the popular pressure for increased access as a social demand or a need that had to be met; or it might look to other countries for insight into whether more open access should be allowed. Neither of these approaches would question whether meeting the demand was justifiable in economic or other terms.

Quantitative projections of what will happen if enrollment were simply allowed to grow (or of growth under a variety of assumptions) are necessary for planning, but as inputs to economic analyses rather than sole indicators of what is needed. Given the heavy burden of educational expenditures in most developing country budgets, it is essential to consider the cost implications of a policy change before implementing it. A useful tool for quantitative projections is a simple flow model based on extrapolations of present or assumed rates of continuation through the system. Such a model was constructed for the Malaysian education system by the writer in 1971.[8] The model was used to indicate the quantitative and cost implications of different rates of access to Form IV.

The choices regarding access to upper secondary were rather narrowly bounded. The upper limit was on the order of 60 percent of candidates, the rate that prevailed prior to the surge in lower secondary enrollment. Rates of admission or levels of access higher than 60 percent were not considered because of high costs, ultimate limits on entry to Form VI and the university, and an intuitive understanding of the problem of overproduction at the Form V level. The lower bound was on the order of 50 percent. Table 4.2 shows the change in the admissions rate between 1965 and 1970. When the rate fell below 50 percent, popular pressure tended to become intense. Some observers advised holding admissions at the same absolute numbers that prevailed before enrollment increases at the lower secondary level. This would have reduced the access rate below 50 percent and perpetuated the elitist nature of academic upper secondary education. Malaysian policy makers, sensitive to political pressures and questions of equity, tended to view 50 percent as an effective minimum rate of admissions. Table 4.3 indicates the quantitative implications of these two levels of access.

Enrollment at the upper secondary level (Forms IV and V) would rise from approximately 90,000 in 1970 to 120,000 in 1975 if access were limited to 50 percent of Form III graduates. The more liberal access rate of 60 percent would lead to enrollment of 144,000 by 1975, as shown in Table 4.3 or a 20 percent difference in total enrollment at the end of the period. Data from the flow model indicate that nearly

TABLE 4.2

Recent Trend in Continuation Rate:
Form III to Form IV

Form III			Form IV	Continuation Rate
1965	to		1966	0.61
1966	to		1967	0.66
1967	to		1968	0.51
1968	to		1969	0.50
1969	to		1970	0.45

Source: Calculated from Table 4.1.

TABLE 4.3

Alternative Projections of Upper Secondary
Enrollment

	Assumption 1 limited (50%) rate of continuation to Form IV	Assumption 2 liberal (60%) rate of continuation to Form IV
1970	89,703	89,703
1971	91,492	101,086
1972	99,443	119,331
1973	109,580	131,496
1974	117,518	141,021
1975	120,194	144,231

Source: Derived from two runs of the flow model discussed in Appendix C.

10,000 more Form V graduates would enter the labor market in 1975 under the more liberal access policy.*

---

*The data on graduates entering the labor market refer to the number of students who would not continue to Form VI and make no allowances for labor force participation rates among seventeen-year-olds not in school.

What would be the cost implications of the alternative policies? Again the flow model makes it possible to consider the effects of a single policy change, holding other assumptions constant. Table 4.4 shows the recurrent and capital costs that would result under the 50 percent and 60 percent access assumptions. The more liberal access policy would lead to additional recurrent costs of between $4 million and $5 million per year by the end of the projection period.* In comparison with total projected recurrent costs of $23.4 million, this is a substantial increase. In comparison with recurrent costs of $372 million for all enrollment (primary through Form VI in 1975), on the other hand, such an increase is not overwhelming. In terms of capital costs, the lower access rate would imply average annual capital costs of $2.1 million to provide for increasing enrollment (assuming a low capital cost per pupil place due to double session use of school buildings).[9] The higher access rate would require an average capital outlay of $3.9 million per year (using the same unit cost assumptions). This again would be within the realm of feasibility, representing a difference of perhaps 2 percent in the annual capital budget for all education. Note that both projections of capital costs reflect the wave effect of rapid increases in enrollment as a result of the earlier policy change, with required annual outlays declining in later years.

Malaysia could afford such increases in absolute terms (although the sum of a number of such "marginal" increases in cost would have a significant impact on the budget). Projections of the costs implied indicated that the higher access rate would be feasible in budget terms.† The question whether it would be economically and socially desirable is, however, a separate issue; as will be discussed in the following sections.

---

*Three Malaysian dollars equalled one U.S. dollar at the time. All future references are to Malaysian dollars.

†This discussion of the quantitative and cost implications of alternative access policies has omitted from consideration their effects on higher levels of education, an important related issue. If the access rate for entry into Form VI were not changed, the flow model indicates that total Form VI enrollment would reach 16,500 under assumption 1 and 19,800 under the liberal-access assumption 2. This in turn would affect demand for university places. If entry into Form VI were held to the lower absolute numbers admitted in the past, despite increased access to Forms IV and V, two things would happen: popular pressure for access to Form VI would increase and the number of Form V graduates entering the labor market would rise.

TABLE 4.4

Alternative Projections of Costs of Upper
Secondary Education
(in thousands of Malaysian dollars)

	Recurrent Costs		Capital Costs	
	Assumption 1	Assumption 2	Assumption 1	Assumption 2
1971	17,841	19,712	617	3,827
1972	19,391	23,270	2,743	6,925
1973	21,368	25,642	3,498	4,197
1974	22,916	27,499	2,738	3,286
1975	23,438	28,125	923	1,007

Note: The alternative assumptions are the same as in Table
4.3. Three Malaysian dollars equalled one American dollar in 1970.

Source: Recurrent costs derived from the flow model. Capital
costs calculated from net increases in enrollment (Table 4.3) times
a capital cost of $345 per double session place, as estimated by
Vickery and Sheath, "Secondary General School Buildings in Malaysia,"
(Colombo: ARISBR, 1971), p. 35.

THE FINDINGS OF MANPOWER AND
RATE-OF-RETURN STUDIES

The manpower study conducted in Malaysia differed from the
model of manpower planning presented in Chapter 2 in that no data
were gathered on the education of workers in the labor force. For
this reason, estimates of educational needs based upon the estimated
occupational demand were even more tenuous than in the usual manpower planning approach. Other problems with the survey were that
it excluded all smallholder agriculture, much of the commercial
sector, and all firms below a minimum size. In all some 44 percent
of the Malaysian labor force was excluded from the survey. Projections of occupational requirements were based upon output estimates
for ten economic sectors. Occupations were categorized as follows:

1. Professional and managerial occupations
   a. Technical
   b. Business specialists
   c. Administrative and managerial

    d.   Agricultural
    e.   Educators
2. Subprofessional Occupations
    a.   Technical
    b.   Administrative and others
    c.   Educators
3. Clerical workers
4. Skilled workers
    a.   White collar
    b.   Blue collar
5. Unskilled workers

Table 4.5 shows the occupational profile of the Malaysian labor force in 1965 according to this categorization scheme.

      Analyses based upon these data tended to draw strong relationships between the very broad occupational categories and educational needs, as follows:

Occupational Classification	Assumed Education Level
Professional and managerial	University level
Subprofessional	Technical education
Clerical	Secondary general or commercial education
Skilled: White-collar	Technical education
Blue-collar	Vocational education
Unskilled	Primary or lower secondary

      When growth of the ten economic sectors was projected (with allowances for productivity changes), the occupational profiles in each sector were applied to the net changes in employment and estimates of educational demand were derived. On the basis of such an analysis, World Bank specialists concluded:

> The Government's education program (1968-1972) . . .
> appears from projections based on currently available
> information to be out of balance. If general secondary
> education facilities were expanded in West Malaysia
> on the lines of this program, the annual output of graduates from 5th to 6th forms by 1975 is estimated to be at
> least three times as much as could be absorbed by the
> labor market thereupon or after training; and even if
> these facilities were not expanded, the output of such
> graduates at the current rate is still likely to be more
> than will be required by 1975. On the other hand, even

TABLE 4.5

Distribution of Employed Labor Force in West Malaysia by Sectors
and Occupational Categories, 1965

	Estate agriculture	Mining and quarrying	Manufacturing	Construction	Electrical supply	Commerce	Transport storage and communication	Other services (private sector)	Public services[f]	Education[g]	Total
Professional/Managerial	2,680	1,120	2,690	890	280	1,780	1,120	1,020	3,410	1,990	16,980
Technical	90	620	520	440	230	290	90	810	1,240	–	4,330
Business specialists[a]	–	120	330	40	30	280	40	30	330	10	1,210
Admin. & mgr'l.	2,590	380	1,720	410	20	1,190	990	180	1,650	190	9,320
Agricultural[b]	–	–	120	–	–	20	–	–	190	–	330
Educators	–	–	–	–	–	–	–	–	–	1,790	1,790
Subprofessional	3,200	1,060	9,230	920	280	15,350	840	1,000	9,970	59,010	100,860
Technical[c]	680	430	890	712	250	350	40	830	6,950	–	11,130
Admin. & others	2,520	630	8,340	210	30	15,000	800	170	3,020	190	30,910
Educators	–	–	–	–	–	–	–	–	–	58,820	58,820
Clerical[d]	5,940	1,960	13,900	2,100	1,260	9,850	3,630	420	15,130	2,460	56,650
Skilled	15,190	16,780	53,010	30,130	4,140	6,940	22,650	850	59,050	1,070	209,810
White collar workers[e]	1,340	1,080	7,310	1,330	520	4,160	1,250	470	40,030	470	57,960
Blue collar workers	13,850	15,700	45,700	28,800	3,620	2,780	21,400	380	19,020	600	151,850
Others	249,990	40,080	94,170	75,960	4,040	241,080	61,760	150,710	95,440	8,800	1,022,030
Total	277,000	61,000	173,000	110,000	10,000	275,000	90,000	154,000	183,000	73,330	1,406,330[h]

aIncludes, among others, economists, statisticians, accountants and auditors.
bIncludes veterinarians, biologists, agronomists, silviculturists, horticulturists, and related scientists.
cIncludes agricultural staff at subprofessional level.
dIncludes clerks and sales personnel.
eIncludes, among others, stenos, typists, bookkeepers, and so on.
fExcludes the education sector.
gIncludes the education sector in the private sector.
hThe estimate of the total employed labor force as of mid-1965 is 2,518,000 of which about 1.1 million was accounted for by those employed in smallholder agriculture.

Source: Manpower Survey, 1965: States of Malaya (Kuala Lumpur: Malaysian Department of Statistics, 1966).

if vocational, agricultural and technical education facilities
are expanded to the extent [now planned] the annual output of graduates from these types of schools by 1975 is
estimated to come on average to only one-fourth of the
needed output.[10]

Note that the bank estimated that, even if the output of Form V
(upper secondary) and Form VI (university-preparatory) did not increase beyond their 1968 levels, there would be three times as many
graduates of these levels as could be absorbed by the labor market;
and that the planned expansion of vocational education—a 383 percent
increase during the First Malaysia Plan period—would still satisfy
only one fourth of the needed output of vocational graduates.

These assessments of severe imbalance between educational
outputs and educational/occupational demand assumed a strong relationship between the clerical and skilled blue-collar occupations on the
one hand and academic secondary education and vocational education,
respectively, on the other. In the absence of educational profiles of
the existing labor force, the bank assumed that 50 percent of the
skilled blue-collar category would require formal vocational preparation. Data from the Socio-Economic Survey conducted two years later
indicated that this was a highly unrealistic assumption. Analysis of
the educational profile of an occupational category corresponding to
"skilled blue-collar" (ILO/SOC: "Craftsmen and Production Process
Workers") showed that only 19 percent had any secondary education
at all in 1967, while only a fraction of 1 percent had formal vocational
preparation.* Even if data on the educational profiles of the labor
force had been available, it would have been difficult to project the
demand for formal vocational education. Malaysia had had very few
vocational schools prior to the mid-nineteen sixties, yet somehow
152,000 skilled blue-collar workers were employed in a category
supposedly requiring a high proportion of vocational graduates. Extrapolating future needs on the basis of manpower assumptions would
have required much arbitrary guesswork.

While the example above is an extreme case of overestimation
of formal educational needs, and is based upon a manpower study that
had many inherent weaknesses, it illustrates some of the problems

---

*Data are from provisional tabulations of the Socio-Economic
Survey of Households, Employment and Unemployment Tables, Table
31.0. 0(a). Among the Craftsmen and Production Process Workers
Category, 12.32 percent had lower secondary education; 4.60 percent
upper secondary; 1.7 percent Form VI; and 0.04 percent teachers or
technical college.

of the manpower approach discussed earlier: the difficulty of trans-
lating occupational demand estimates into educational requirements,
a tendency for manpower studies to be biased toward high-skill needs
and demand for formal preparation (particularly vocational education),
and a disregard of the possibilities for skill substitution and on-job
skill development. It also illustrates another point regarding the
orientation of the major planning approaches. The only policy information that such studies usually produce concerns the levels of
enrollment in different sorts of education (in this case, very broad
aggregates). In terms of providing information bearing upon the
access question, the manpower data indicated a problem of over production of upper secondary graduates and a perceived shortfall in vocational outputs. This was useful in itself, since it called attention to
the problem. But it does not indicate any alternative courses of action
other than shifting enrollment.

It would be possible to discuss the Malaysian Manpower Survey
at greater length. (The issue of demand for vocational education will
arise again in the following chapter.) For the purposes of this chapter,
however, it is sufficient to say that the manpower data (and estimates
of educational need based upon them) indicated overproduction of
Form V graduates. The policy recommendation one would make on
this basis alone would be to curtail access to the upper secondary
level; perhaps even below the 50 percent level.

Let us consider what the rate-of-return approach to planning
indicates regarding access to upper secondary. Analysis of rates of
return by O. D. Hoerr, based on income, age, and education data
from the 1967 Socio-Economic Survey yielded the internal rates of
return show in Table 4.6.

One of the first observations that one makes from the table is
that the returns are, with the exception of university education, relatively high and quite closely grouped. It is also apparent that investment in secondary education yields higher returns than investment in
primary and university education. This information conflicts directly
with the manpower findings (and especially with the interpretations
placed upon the manpower data). A major imbalance in educational
outputs, such as overproduction of general secondary education,
would produce wide differences in returns to investment, with low
returns to the surplus form of education. The relatively closely
grouped returns and the high return to secondary education found by
Hoerr indicate that a major imbalance did not in fact exist in 1967-68,
and that secondary education (all levels) was a good investment from
either a private or a social standpoint.

Blaug remarks on the possibility of divergences between manpower and rate-of-return findings: "If we get different answers from
rate of return calculations than from manpower forecasts, it may be

TABLE 4.6

Internal Rates of Return to Investments in
Education in Malaysia, 1967-68

	Cumulative		Marginal	
Education level	Social returns	Private returns	Social returns	Private returns
Primary	8.2	12.9	8.2	12.9
Forms I-II	11.9	17.0	15.6	21.1
Forms III-IV	13.6	17.6	15.3	18.9
Form VI	13.2	17.1	12.8	15.6
University	9.5	16.0	5.8	11.4

Source: O. D. Hoerr, "Education, Income, and Equity in Malaysia," Economic Development and Cultural Change, 21, no. 2 (January, 1973): 260.

that (a) earnings are divorced from the marginal productivity of labor, (b) the costs of education are artificially inflated, (c) future rates of return will diverge from present rates or (d) the manpower forecasts are wrong."[11] The problem in Malaysia seemed to be of type (c); but the high returns to secondary education, which was supposed to be in surplus, indicated that (d) held true as well. As noted earlier, most rate-of-return studies reveal the relative scarcities of different types of education at a point in time—that is, points on the demand curves for different sorts of education—and do not indicate what will happen if supplies of education change markedly in the future. The 1967 Socio-Economic Survey provided data on the income and education of the then-employed labor force, prior to the rapid expansion of lower and upper secondary enrollment and outputs. It would be expected that a major change in the quantities of each sort of graduates entering the labor market would influence the marginal returns strongly.*

*Use of Dougherty's approach (as discussed in Ch. 1) with estimated elasticities of substitution, would tend to overcome this problem. The difference between the social and private rates of return shown in Table 4.6 indicates why popular pressure for access to upper secondary could increase even though the marginal social

Hoerr is cognizant of the problem of changing relative returns and uses separate data on unemployment rates among new entrants to the labor force (which were high for secondary graduates) to qualify his rate of return findings:

> Unemployment is already high and growing for people
> with secondary education; given the undifferentiated
> nature of skills at this level, the combination of high
> returns and high unemployment is inherently unstable.
> The probability of declines in social profitability is, of
> course, greatly reinforced by continuation of secondary
> expansion—which also has implications for returns else-
> where.[12]

In other words the high returns to secondary education observed for those educated before 1967 must be qualified by indications of growing unemployment among secondary graduates, which tend to give greater credence to the manpower study's findings.

The policy conclusions one can draw regarding access are thus ambiguous. From a superficial examination of the rate-of-return data, one would conclude that liberal access (that is, the 60 percent rate or above) would be economically sound. When this information is augmented by data on increasing unemployment among recent secondary graduates, however, the desirability of further expansion appears questionable. (Such a conjunction of rate-of-return analysis with other sorts of policy information may often produce greater insight). The high returns in the past cast some doubt upon the assumptions regarding manpower demand, but the manpower data tend to be in agreement with the information on unemployment of secondary graduates. Three points raised in Chapter 2 are thus demonstrated:

> (1) There are inherent problems with the usual
> approaches to planning that limit their usefulness in
> providing information for decision makers;
> (2) The information produced, even assuming the
> technical problems away, relates to a limited set of
> policy variables (that is, enrollment changes) and over-
> looks important lower-level factors; and
> (3) Other sorts of analysis and other kinds of data
> (in this case examination of unemployment rates outside

---

returns were falling. Individuals make educational choices on the basis of private returns, which are virtually always higher than social returns.

the frameworks of either manpower or rate-of-return analysis) can improve the information on which to base choices. Let us consider these three points further.

We have thus far touched upon only one problem of rate-of-return analysis in connection with the Malaysian study: The inability of the rate-of-return approach to deal with major changes in supplies of different sorts of education. Hoerr deals with this problem by looking at recent data on unemployment among certain groups. Other methodologies may also make it possible to overcome this problem. There are other problems with the rate-of-return approach that are also illustrated. The categorization scheme (as shown in Table 4.6) is crude. Returns from Forms III and IV are lumped together and returns from Form V are not differentiated from Form VI. This problem stems from the way the basic data were gathered in the Socio-Economic Survey. While survey data might be gathered on more useful educational categories, there are other limitations that are not so easily overcome. Information on alternative ways of adjusting the content of upper secondary education would require that data be gathered on graduates of vocational schools, the arts and science streams (separately), and the "technical schools" that approximated comprehensive education. But broad social surveys cannot gather such specific data on small groups in the society without altering their sampling methodology and loading their questionnaires with much detail. Different means of gathering data on the income and employment effects of different alternatives would perhaps be possible, as will be discussed later. Other problems include the heterogeneous nature of education as a variable to explain income differences and the method of adjusting income differences for the effects of other variables related to education.[13] Possible analytical approaches investigating the same income and employment variables as manpower and rate-of-return studies but with an orientation toward comparison of internal policy alternatives will be considered later in this chapter.

INTERRACIAL EQUITY AND ACCESS TO
UPPER SECONDARY EDUCATION

Educational policy makers in Malaysia were concerned with other factors in addition to rates of return and manpower needs as they considered the question of access. Probably the most important factor in their preference structure in 1970 was the role of education in creating greater social and economic equality in their multiethnic society. In May of 1969, Malaysia experienced serious racial conflicts that deeply affected the nation. As one result, most government pronouncements, including the Second Malaysia Plan, stressed the theme of racial harmony.[14] The introduction to the plan begins: "National unity is the over-riding objective of the country. A stage has been reached where greater emphasis must be placed on social integration and more equitable distribution of income and opportunities for national unity and progress."[15]

Equality of educational opportunity was a key issue and the education system was viewed as an important instrument for redressing the imbalances in social and economic well-being between Malays and non-Malays. The opening statement of the plan's education program gives highest priority to achieving the goal of national unity, which, in this context, meant greater opportunity for the Malays: "Program improvements in 1971-1975 will . . . concentrate on . . . (i) consolidation of the education system to promote national integration and unity. . . ."[16]

One major policy step called for year-by-year elimination of English as a medium of instruction.* The question of access to the various levels of education, while not as dramatic as the language policy, was also of central importance. Equity and access are interrelated in various ways. (1) Most obviously, the numbers of Malays and non-Malays admitted (and the proportions of candidates admitted from each group) involved equity questions and was politically sensitive. (2) The relative quality of educational services offered in each medium also raised equity issues. (3) The effects of education on lifetime opportunities for students were assumed to be positive (although research in other countries raised questions regarding this assumption). Given this assumption, however, the relative efficiency with which the two educational media accomplished their academic ends (that is, improving performance on examinations) became important from an equity standpoint. Planning, research, and economic analysis could provide some information in all of these areas.

Looking first at the quantitative aspects of equity of access, the education system had attempted to provide compensation for socio-economic differences for some time. The Malay language

---

*Within some seven years, the language policy change would result in elimination of the English language stream at the upper secondary level. For the medium-term future, though, policy makers had to consider the question of access to two separate language media. The language policy change was one of the most important policy decisions in Malaysian educational history, with profound equity implications. A full consideration of the language question, however, would lead far beyond the scope of the present section.

medium served mainly the Malay population while English medium enrollment consisted primarily of Chinese and Indian students.* The "promotion pass" rates set for the LCE exam in English and the SRP exam in Malay differed; passing grades that admitted the candidates to upper secondary were set lower in the Malay medium. As a result, some Malays were promoted with SRP scores that were inferior to the LCE scores of non-Malay students who were not promoted. If this seems grossly inequitable in its own right, two points should be noted. First, the quality of lower-level preparation in the predominately rural Malay medium schools was inferior to lower-level preparation in the English medium; thus to require exactly the same levels of achievement and competence in the two media would discriminate against the Malays. Second, the wastage rates at lower levels in the Malay medium were higher than in English medium, even with automatic promotions. Thus those candidates attaining Form III and sitting for the exam had already been prescreened in a sense. To admit a lower proportion of Malay candidates because of a purely merit criterion would further restrict the already limited enrollment ratios among the Malay population.

Table 4.7 shows enrollment by race and sex as a percent of the population in the age group corresponding to each educational level. (The breakdown by sex permits separate assessment of the influence of Malay cultural attitudes on education for women.) This table shows that enrollment ratios for Malays are consistently lower than for the Chinese and Indian populations.† The table also reveals the effect of compensatory admissions to upper secondary. While the enrollment ratio for Malays at the lower secondary level is 78 percent as high as the non-Malay ratio, it rises to 90 percent of the non-Malay ratio at upper secondary.

There is an important political dimension to the relationship between the differential pass rates and the overall access question. Such compensation raises political reactions among the groups that the compensatory policy works against. The more narrowly access

---

*Some Malay students made the language change after the sixth grade (at a cost of one year spent in the "remove" year of language transition) and continued their secondary education in English. They tended to be handicapped, however, by less adequate lower-level preparation and less sure command of English.

†Hoerr notes the difficulty of comparing data from disparate sources: enrollment data are from the Ministry of Education, while population data are from the Department of Statistics. He feels that Malay enrollment ratios are actually somewhat lower than those shown here.

TABLE 4.7

Enrollment Ratios by Level, by Race and Sex, 1967
(% of age-eligible population)

Educational Level	Malays		Non-Malays	
	Males	Females	Males	Females
Primary	85.4	79.3	94.7	85.3
Lower secondary	55.3	36.5	71.0	50.1
Upper secondary	18.1	13.5	20.0	23.1
Form VI	1.7	0.8	2.4	1.6

Source: Hoerr, Economic Development and Cultural Change
(January, 1973), op. cit., p. 269. Population data are derived from a
special tabulation of the Socio-Economic Survey performed by the
Department of Statistics; enrollment data are from the EPRD.

is limited in general, the more salient the policy of compensation
becomes. As a result, the political pressures against the policy
become more intense. In short, it is easier to admit Malays to upper
secondary on a compensatory basis in the context of a liberal policy
of access. Further, a policy of more open access simply permits
more Malays to advance to upper secondary on an absolute basis, as
well as on a relative basis. This pragmatic political point had an
important influence upon the overall access question.

Arguments against more liberal access were based upon a
perceived overproduction of Form V graduates. In the light of employment policies instituted after the racial disturbances of 1969, these
arguments did not apply as strongly, if at all, to Malay medium
graduates. New government policies called for greater employment
of Malays in the public and private sectors. This created an anomalous
situation in which there were more positions open (particularly at
middle levels and upward) than there were Malays with educational
qualifications to fill them. The findings of aggregate manpower
studies were thus overtaken by events. The arguments concerning
equity and access were extraordinarily complex and this discussion
must necessarily pass over many important related questions. In
general, however, equity considerations introduced another perspective
on the access question and generally favored more liberal access.

There are relationships between who enters a level such as
upper secondary and what happens to them once they get there. Various
bits of data from the secondary school survey cast light upon this

issue. The survey provided data not previously available on the distribution of educational services (that is, the relative "quality" of education) between the two media.* Of the many variables included in the survey, only a few were found to be significantly related to the dependent variable: a longitudinally-measured indicator of educational performance based upon examination scores.[17] Some of the significant variables have a direct bearing upon the questions of equity and access.

The variable with greatest explanatory power was the student's entering score on the LCE or SRP examinations.[18] In other words, while upper secondary school inputs could have significant effects upon the student's educational achievement, earlier experiences gained both inside and out of school had a greater effect. This is not surprising nor should it be interpreted as an indication that schooling is fruitless; school inputs did have an effect. It does have policy implications regarding access. Opening access very widely at this and higher levels is unlikely to have much impact on the academic performance of marginal and submarginal students.† Thus a policy of completely open access is not likely to improve the lot of disadvantaged students in academic terms. (On the other hand, if simply passing through the system and obtaining educational credentials improved employability and income for the disadvantaged, this would be an argument for open access; at least until employers discovered that the credentials were often meaningless.) Another implication of the strong relationship between entering scores and the performance variable is that policies aimed at achieving equal education for the Malays should concentrate first on improving the quality of lower levels of schooling.

The explanatory power of the entering score variable gives rise to another point: this variable's explanatory power differed between media. "47% of the total variance in academic attainment for students instructed in the Malay language and 60% for English

---

*See Appendix B of this study for a description of the survey, its variables, and methodology. The descriptive data indicated that Malay schools, particularly rural schools, were not as well provided with some educational inputs as English schools. On the other hand, Malay schools were better supplied with some inputs that are generally considered important for educational quality. The issue was: which variables make a difference?

†Admitting many submarginal students, who would be unlikely to profit academically from the experience, would very probably have an unfavorable effect upon the quality of education for more able students.

language students can be explained by an extremely simple model using the student's entering achievement score as the sole independent variable."[19] Beebout notes that this is surprising. "It implies that there is more opportunity for a student to increase or decrease his achievement in a Malay medium rather than an English medium school. This, in turn, implies greater 'equality of educational opportunity' in the Malay medium system."[20] The entering score is a powerful predictor of academic success, which leads to the conclusion that some limitation on access was desirable to avoid overburdening the system with students who could probably never do well academically. But the lower explanatory power of the entering score variable in the Malay medium indicates that it might be justifiable to admit Malay students from lower on the grade scale than non-Malay students. There is a need for further investigation into the reasons for the difference, but is is a thought-provoking finding (which provides some justification after the fact for the policy of differential pass rates).

Some school input variables were significantly associated with academic performance. The most important of these were teacher-related variables: years of experience and levels of academic preparation. Here the provision of inputs differed between media, with Malay medium schools being less well supplied with qualified teachers. Table 4.8 shows that in 57 percent of rural Malay schools and 47 percent of urban Malay schools less than 10 percent of the teachers were graduates of appropriate teacher training courses. On the other hand, only 10 percent of rural and 11 percent of urban English schools had less than 10 percent graduate teachers. Since 79 percent of Malay schools are classified as rural as compared with 28 percent of English schools, the degree of difference in supply of graduate teachers is seen to be more pronounced. In the sense of reducing inequality between media, provision of more graduate teachers to Malay schools would offer relatively high benefits.

Teacher experience is another significant variable. Table 4.9 shows the distribution of schools by the average number of years' teaching experience of their staffs. An average of less than five years' experience implies that a substantial proportion of the teaching force consists of new, inexperienced teachers. In many developing countries, it is difficult to maintain experienced teachers in rural areas. Rural schools are staffed by recent graduates, who move to the city as soon as their obligatory period of service where assigned is completed. The data in Table 4.9 reveal such a pattern. The survey data also reveal that in 36 percent of rural Malay schools, over 50 percent of the teachers had less than two years' experience. Among rural English medium schools, only 12 percent of the schools had such a high proportion of inexperienced teachers.

TABLE 4.8

Distribution of Schools by Percent Graduate Teachers
in Upper Secondary Schools, by Medium,
Urban vs. Rural

Percent of graduate teachers	Malay medium		English medium	
	rural	urban	rural	urban
0 - 9	57	43	19	11
10-19	21	29	19	19
20-29	11		6	19
30-39	7	14	44	14
40-49	—	—	13	—
50 and over	4	14		38

+

Source: H. S. Beebout, "EPRD Secondary School Survey:
Preliminary Report," (Kuala Lumpur: Education Planning and Research Division, 1971), p. 37.

TABLE 4.9

Distribution of Schools by Average Years' Experience
of Teachers, by Medium, Urban and Rural

Average years' experience	Malay medium		English medium	
	rural	urban	rural	urban
0.0-4.9 years	44	25	38	18
5.0-6.9 years	26	50	50	21
7.0-8.9 years	22	25	13	32
9.0-more	7	—	—	29

Source: H. S. Beebout, "The Production Surface for Academic
Achievement," (unpublished Ph.D. dissertation, University of Wisconsin
at Madison, 1972), p. 121.

Other school inputs have traditionally been considered important determinants of academic success. Among these are the quality of various educational facilities (buildings, libraries, laboratories, and so on), expenditures per pupil and class size.[21] These inputs were not significantly associated with the index of academic performance, which raises a series of questions. Have educational funds been spent unwisely? What would be the most effective means of achieving greater equality between the Malay and English mediums of instruction? What would it cost to achieve equality of educational opportunity if resources were concentrated on the important inputs? How much could be saved on the less important inputs without having damaging effects on performance? Beebout addresses some of these points, but he emphasizes that findings of a single empirical study such as this should be used with caution and further investigation of apparent relationships should be conducted before action programs are undertaken. The study raises a wide array of interesting questions concerning the efficiency of the education system and the equality of provision of educational services. It illustrates the feasibility of gathering performance-related data and using them to stimulate policy thinking. It also illustrates the sorts of economic analysis that can be brought to bear on efficiency and equity questions at lower levels of optimization.

THE DECISIONS ON ACCESS AND THE CHOICES THAT FOLLOWED

The manpower and rate-of-return approaches produced conflicting findings regarding the access question. Data on recent employment and unemployment rates among secondary school graduates indicated some apparent overproduction and tended to favor tighter limitations on access. The desire to provide greater educational opportunities for Malays (plus changes in the manpower and employment situation due to government policy initiatives) tipped the balance back toward more liberal access, at least for Malays. And political considerations probably persuaded some policy makers that it would be possible to do more for the Malays in the context of a generally open access policy.

What course did Malaysian policy makers take in fact? The Second Malaysia Plan projects upper secondary academic enrollment to reach 140,000 in 1975.[22] This is almost as high as the projection of 144,000 based upon a 60 percent access rate, and well above the level of 120,000 that would result from a 50 percent rate (see Table 4.3 above). In other words, the policy implied is one of relatively liberal access to upper secondary academic schools.

It would be incorrect to claim that Malaysian policy makers arrived at their choices through a conscious application of the principles set forth in this and earlier chapters. On the other hand most of the studies and information considered in this chapter were available to decision makers, at least in preliminary form, at the time the Second Malaysia Plan was completed. The decision-making style was far from an orderly and rational process, but was rather a disjointed process in which different interests raised contrary and competing views. The policy studies cited here did not lead to explicit systems analyses and clear answers, but the mere existence of the data and awareness of the various questions raised by the studies may have had an effect on the ultimate policy choice. In any event, the policy chosen tended toward liberal access at a level slightly below the 60 percent upper bound.

Given that a relatively liberal access policy was chosen, could economic analysis provide any information on what to do next? What about the growing unemployment among secondary graduates that Hoerr observed? Could analysis indicate ways in which increased numbers of graduates might be assured of higher incomes and employability (or the costs of education might be reduced) so as to affect the rates of return in the future? Let us look again at the nature of the upper secondary level that was to be expanded.

Upper secondary education followed the elitist British model of preparing students for the next higher level of education, in this case the university-preparatory Form VI. Since access to Form VI was strictly limited and likely to remain so, a large portion of the academically prepared upper secondary graduates entered the labor market prepared only for white-collar jobs. As noted, there were several alternative policies that might have the effect of increasing their employability and income and resolving the problem of over-production. Since it was decided to expand access, which of the alternatives—vocational education, greater science enrollment, or comprehensive education—offered the greatest potential benefits? Vocational education will be considered in the next chapter. What could analysis tell us about the desirability of comprehensive education or increased science enrollment?

Shifting Enrollment to the Science Stream

Enrollment in the science stream was known to be very low in comparison to arts stream enrollment, but until the secondary school survey no quantitative picture of the balance was available. Definition of what constituted a science stream student was difficult because all students studied some science as part of the core curriculum. Beebout's criterion was based upon the number of students who "sat

95

for a minimum combination of [three] science subjects."[23] On this basis science enrollment amounted to 0.3 percent of total Malay medium and 13.7 percent of English medium enrollment.[24] As reported by the schools in the survey questionnaire, science stream enrollment was considerably higher: 23 percent in the Malay medium and 34 percent in English medium.[25] The reasons for the differences were apparently two: the schools reported Form IV enrollment in science and a substantial number of students abandon the science course after one year; and of those students who complete the two years, a portion decide not to sit for the minimum of three science tests. Official policy statements recommended an increase in science stream enrollment to 60 percent in both mediums, which was more of a wish than a feasible target. A representative statement on the need for increased science enrollment was made by the Director General of Education:

> We have seen that the economic and social progress achieved by advanced countries have been primarily due to the application of science and technology to all aspects of their everyday life. If we are to progress and keep abreast of the dictates of the rapidly changing world, a similar program will have to be adopted by us because the accent of today's world is on science and technology. I regard this as essentially a problem for education. . . . The education system has to be sufficiently geared so that its output is consonant with the economic needs of the country. Today the country needs more blue-collar workers, more technicians, engineers, doctors, scientists and the like.[26]

The assumption that science graduates were more employable and earned higher incomes than arts graduates was untested because no information on their comparative experience had been gathered. This was an area where economic analysis—in this case of the relative benefits of the arts and science streams—would have made it possible to base policy on fact rather than conjecture. Due to the small numbers of science graduates in the labor force, large-scale social surveys would be unlikely to produce reliable information on comparative earnings and employment. Thus special purpose longitudinal surveys of graduates in each category—as recommended in Chapter 3—would have been necessary to produce data for analysis.

On the cost side, little was known about the relative costs of science and arts education. (Recall that even the numbers in each stream were not clearly known.) A rough estimate by the writer of the cost of a science pupil over and above the cost of an arts pupil

is $72 per year.* While this is on the order of a 20 to 25 percent
increase over annual public recurrent and capital costs of upper
secondary, it is of course a smaller increase over total costs (including
out of pocket costs paid by the student plus income foregone).† In
comparison with the cumulative social costs of producing a Form V
graduate, which Hoerr's data indicate to be on the order of $5,600,
the added cost of $144 for two years of science enrollment is less
than 3 percent.[27] The scarcity of relevant data for analysis of the
science education alternative is revealing, particularly since Malaysia
is better supplied with data than most developing countries. It is
enlightening to explore the implications of these costs, even on such
a rough basis at this. (For example, shifting 40,000 pupils or one-
third of total upper secondary enrollment from the arts to the science
stream would increase recurrent costs by $2,480,000 annually.) We
will return to these figures later in comparing the science enrollment
alternative with others.

An important qualification on the feasibility and desirability of
shifting enrollment to the science stream is suggested by the secondary
school survey data and anecdotal evidence. Students were reluctant
to enter the science stream, particularly in the Malay medium.
Beebout's analysis indicated that being a science major was associated
with a five point advantage in performance for English medium

_____

*The lack of such cost data is indicative of the need for better
cost analysis. Average recurrent costs per pupil in 1969, based on
the secondary school survey data, were $247 in the Malay medium
and $291 in the English medium. Actual costs in those few English
medium schools with 100 percent science enrollment were very high
and not representative of the costs of science enrollment alone. (These
were the "premier schools" of the country, with many other cost-
augmenting characteristics. Per pupil costs ranged from $600 to
over $700.) Based on capital cost estimates per pupil year from
Vickery and Sheath (op. cit., p. 32), a rough scatter plot analysis of
per pupil costs against science enrollment, and data from the secondary
school survey on science teaching and expendable materials costs
per unit, the following rough estimates were derived: capital cost
addition, $10; additional costs of science teaching, $35; additional
costs for expendable materials, $27; total addition: $72.

†The $72 per year figure assumes that average teacher qualifi-
cations would not change. The costs of providing science education
with fully-qualified teachers, as would be necessary in order to achieve
high quality and the assumed benefits of science education, would
easily increase this figure by a factor of 2.0.

students but science students in the Malay medium suffered a four point disadvantage.[28] This was due to relatively recent introduction of science courses in the Malay medium, shortages of qualified Malay science teachers and texts, and probably counselling of better Malay students to enter the arts stream.[29] Even in the English medium, where the best students were counselled to study science, the demanding science curriculum and difficult examinations tended to hold science enrollment down. Increasing science enrollment would require more than an administrative order. In the Malay medium in particular, it would probably be unadvisable to attempt to increase the proportion of students enrolled in science until preparation was improved in the lower grades and more qualified teachers were available.

Adopting a "Comprehensive Education" Model.

Comprehensive education appeared to offer a means of increasing the number of academic places without overproduction of academically prepared graudates. The concept of comprehensive education was that prevocational courses could be added to the basic academic curriculum, thus providing some exposure to practical material, orientation toward blue-collar occupations and, ultimately, greater employability and income. As appealing as this best-of-both-worlds alternative appeared, it was not without inherent problems. As in the case of the science alternative, no information on benefits was available. It would have been possible to gather income and employment data on graduates of schools very similar to the comprehensive model, but this had not been done. A limited number of upper secondary schools called technical schools offered upper secondary academic education plus some courses in practical subjects.[30] Unlike the vocational schools, which offered an occupation-oriented terminal course that was viewed as a last resort for those who could not enter the academic stream, the technical schools prepared pupils for higher levels of education (often in Form VI technical colleges) and attracted some of the best of each cohort of candidates for upper secondary. Academic schools devoted 100 percent of their curriculum time to academic studies; technical schools divided the time between academic studies (77 percent) and workshop and classroom time devoted to practical studies (23 percent).* Vocational education, by comparison, devoted 53 percent of a slightly longer class week to practical courses. Enrollment in the technical stream was small, amounting to approximately 2 percent of total upper secondary enrollment. A higher than

---

*These figures are from EPRD data. The total time in both cases was twenty-nine hours and forty minutes per week.

average proportion of technical graduates succeeded in entering Form VI, but it would have been possible to study the employment and income experience of those graduates who entered the labor market for information on a form of education very similar to the comprehensive model. This, unfortunately, was not done.

Data on the unit costs of technical education were, again, poor and cost estimates varied widely. It was known that costs were high. Average costs also varied considerably from year to year due to changes in enrollment with relatively constant costs for staff and facilities. An estimate by the writer indicated capital costs of $147 and recurrent costs of $620 per year in 1967, which were well above the costs of academic education, even in the science stream. Other data showed costs of technical schools per pupil varying between $649 and $919 between 1963 and 1966.[31] The ministry's statistical publication showed that "grants to secondary technical education" (which included only recurrent costs) were $662 per pupil in 1967. Costs were expected to rise to $1,063 in 1968.[32]

The reasons for the high costs included: (1) higher capital costs for more science laboratories, practical workshops, and equipment for practical courses; (2) costs of more highly qualified teachers than in most secondary schools, including specialist teachers in practical subjects; (3) costs for expendable materials; (4) relatively low utilization of facilities and staff time. Another cost, which is not reflected in these figures, was the cost of boarding. Since only a few technical schools existed in the country, students from distant locations required expensive hostel facilities. In comparison with an average figure of approximately $270 per pupil year, the cost of $770 for technical education represented a major increase, amounting to $1,000 for the two years required to produce a graduate. In cumulative cost terms, this would mean an 18 percent increase over the total (public and private) costs of producing an academic upper secondary graduate.

The costs of the few technical schools that existed were probably higher than the costs of a more broadly implemented comprehensive education scheme due to various cost-raising characteristics of the technical schools, which provided highset-quality education to a select group of students. The benefits of technical education (if they had been known) would also probably be higher than benefits of many comprehensive schools. Despite possible differences between the existing technical schools and the proposed alternative, it would have been possible to gather useful information for systematic economic analysis of the comprehensive education alternative.

The most serious data gap in the case of both alternatives was information on their income and employment effects. In the absence of such data, it is still possible to perform a rough sort of economic analysis that may provide information on their relative desirability in comparison with each other and with academic upper secondary education. If we turn benefit-cost analysis around backward, so to speak, and apply it to this micro-analytical question, we can determine the present value of lifetime earnings streams that would be necessary to justify the added investments in these alternatives. Since the costs of the alternatives are known, and Hoerr's data indicates the rate of return to academic upper secondary education, it is a fairly simple matter to determine what the present value of alternative benefits would have to be in order to produce a rate of return at least as high as that of academic upper secondary education. With the aid of some strong assumptions, it is also possible to estimate what starting salaries would have to be in order to yield adequate present values to justify the investments.

The standard approach to calculating internal rates of return is to determine the rate of discount (i) that reduces the net benefit stream from the investment to zero in the following equation:

$$V = \sum_{t=1}^{n} \frac{E_t - C_t}{(1+i)^t} \qquad (1)$$

V equals the present value of net benefits, which are the differences in each year between earnings (E) and costs (C). The relevant time period is from ages seventeen (completion of Form V) to sixty-five. In the present case, we can calculate the present value of costs of all alternatives and we know the internal rate of return that Hoerr observed for academic upper secondary (13.6 percent). The present values that would be necessary to justify investment in the alternative are then:

$$\sum_{t=17}^{65} \frac{E_t}{(1.136)^t} = C_t \qquad (2)$$

since V was equal to zero when i equaled 13.6 percent.

The total social costs of producing an academic upper secondary graduate, including public costs, students' out-of-pocket costs and income foregone, were calculated by Hoerr and amount to approximately \$5,600 for the eleven years of schooling.[33] For appropriate comparison with present value of benefits, the year-by-year costs should also be appreciated to a present value of costs. Using a rate of interest of 10 percent (Hoerr's assumed opportunity cost of capital in Malaysia) the present value of total social costs of academic upper secondary schooling is $8,570. Rates of return are usually calculated on the basis of incremental costs and benefits associated with adding another level of education but it is somewhat easier and more direct to deal with total cumulative costs and benefits in the present example. Either approach can be correct but cumulative benefits can be more easily related to starting salaries. The present values of the lifetime earnings streams of the two alternatives would have to equal the cost of academic upper secondary plus the incremental costs estimated above, appreciated to present value.*

Present value of academic upper secondary
  benefits: $8,570
"Target" present value of science education: $8,800
"Target" present value of comprehensive
  education: $9,410

In order to interpret these target present value figures operationally, it is necessary to convert them to approximate average starting salaries. This step involves several strong assumptions and has several weaknesses. For one thing, the age-earnings profiles of different occupation/education groups might differ considerably. With a discount rate as high as 13.6 percent, the target starting salaries would be highly sensitive to differences in the phasing of future income benefits. For another, average starting salaries are also highly sensitive to employment rates among the relevant groups, and knowledge of these is limited and imperfect. Another problem with the approach is that Hoerr characterized the observed internal rate of return as "unstable" and found indications that recent cohorts of secondary graduates were not finding ready acceptance in the labor market. Despite these acknowledged weaknesses of the approach, it can provide some useful information.

Blaug notes that age-earnings profiles exhibit considerable regularity, even between different sorts of education and in different countries:

––––––––––––

*The added cost of a science major was $72 per year, assuming no change in average teacher qualifications. If we assume a moderate improvement in teacher qualifications in order to achieve the anticipated income and employment benefits, this cost would be on the order of $110 per year or a total present value of $231 for the two year cycle. Technical education costs of $500 per year were probably "gold plated" and comprehensive education costs could be roughly estimated at $400 per year or a total present value of $840.

1. All profiles, irrespective of the years of schooling or level of education attained, increase with age up
to a maximum point somewhere after forty and then level
off, or in some cases even decline.
2. The higher the educational attainment, the
steeper the rise in earnings throughout the early phases
of working life and usually, although not invariably, the
higher the starting salary.
3. The higher the educational attainment, the later
the year at which maximum earnings are reached and
the higher retirement earnings.[34]

Since we are comparing fairly similar alternatives in the same
country and in a very rough, indicative calculation, we will make
the strong assumption that the shape of the three age-earnings
profiles is very similar. If we further assume that average starting
salaries of the three sets of graduates (that is, salaries of employed
graduates divided by the total number of economically active graduates)
are subject to the same labor market forces, then we can finally
assume that the relationships between the starting salaries associated
with the several alternatives correspond to the relationships between
their target present values. In other words, if the target present
values of science and comprehensive education exceed the present
value of academic upper secondary by 3 percent and 10 percent
respectively, starting salaries of their graduates (adjusted for the
probability of employment) ought to exceed the starting salary of
academic graduates by similar percentages. We can then look to the
labor market to see whether such starting salaries would be within
the realm of reason.

Information on starting salaries was woefully inadequate in
Malaysia. In addition, since average salaries are the product of
earnings of employed graduates and the probability of employment,
and since employment rates fluctuate considerably, they are subject
to considerable variation through time. For the purpose of the present
rough calculation, the figures shown in Table 4.10 provide some
indication of starting salary differentials.

According to the analysis above, the starting salaries of science
graduates should be 3 percent higher than academic graduates and
comprehensive graduates should earn 10 percent more than academic
graduates. These figures imply salary ranges of $165-258 for science
graduates and $176-275 for comprehensive graduates. The ranges
shown in Table 4.10 indicate that such average salaries are in the
realm of possibility. If the implied ranges had been as high as the
starting salary range for Form VI graduates, this would have given
cause to doubt the justifiability of the investments. If surveys of

TABLE 4.10

Earnings Differentials Between Different Education Levels in West Malaysia, 1967

Level of education or skill	Starting salary per month
University honors degree	600-1000
University pass degree	500
Higher school certificate Form VI)	350-400
School certificate (Form V)	160-250
Skilled workers	160-250*
Unskilled workers (outside peasant agriculture)	60-170*
Unskilled workers (in peasant agriculture)	30-45*

*Data are for average salaries of all workers, not starting salaries.

Source: Suffian Report, cited in Eddy Lee, Educational Planning in West Malaysia (Kuala Lumpur: Oxford University Press, 1972), p. 31.

recent graduates of the science stream and the technical schools indicated that their starting salaries fell within these ranges and exceeded those of academic graduates by the target percentages, then decision makers could be reasonably well assured that investments in the alternative forms of education would be at least as sound as investments in academic upper secondary.

There are, as noted, various grounds for criticizing this sort of analysis and various fine points could be elaborated at length. Even though the exercise is rough and sometimes tortured, it illustrates the sorts of information (particularly cost information and some indicators of benefits) that would be needed to provide partial, micro-analytical information to decision makers. It also indicates how the same benefit-cost concepts underlying the rate-of-return approach can be reoriented to compare lower-level alternatives. And finally it shows how complex policy choices can be structured in terms of economic comparisons between alternatives, a "way of looking at problems" that has not often been applied to education sector choices at the operational level. The same data will be used in considering the vocational education alternative in the following chapter.

MODIFYING THE TOOLS OF ECONOMIC ANALYSIS
AND THEIR ORIENTATION

The access policy issue illustrates the need for a variety of applications of economic analysis to the hierarchy of interrelated questions that arose. While the manpower and rate-of-return approaches served to put the issue in broad perspective and identify the possible problem of overproduction of academic graduates, other forms of analysis have been shown to offer useful additional information. The brief notes below examine the several ways in which the basic concept of benefit cost analysis can be oriented toward lower-level choices and other methodologies can perhaps be brought to bear on real policy issues.

(1) Investigation of the income and employment effects of alternative types of education can provide much-needed information on relative benefits of the alternatives. If such investigations were carried out regularly, changes in the way the labor market appreciated alternative forms of education would become apparent. Pilot programs designed specifically to increase income and employability could be tested on the basis of such information. Longitudinal studies of samples of graduates of each type of education would make it possible to identify benefits among small groups of recent graduates, which cannot be reliably measured on the basis of broad social survey data.

(2) Cost-effectiveness analysis, measuring not only income-related benefits but also changes in academic performance are also feasible. The secondary school sample survey made it possible to identify input variables that were significantly related to a performance indicator and measure the performance gain per dollar invested in different inputs.[35] Where no such examination-based measure of performance is available, graduates of alternative educational programs (including, for example, students exposed to different curriculums) can be tracked through later years of schooling and their relative performance monitored by various means (class rankings, teachers' appraisals, wastage rates, and so on). There are many opportunities for asking and answering cost-effectiveness questions and applying economic ways of thinking to internal policy choices.

(3) The comparison of the science and comprehensive education alternatives illustrated the need for (and scarcity of) sound cost data. Inadequate cost information is an all-too-frequent problem in developing countries. Even without relating costs to performance, mere measurement of cost can serve to sharpen policy insights. (Despite much conjecture on the desirability of more science education or the comprehensive education model, no one had gathered good data on what either alternative would cost.) When used together, cost and performance data can operate like a lever and a fulcrum to improve educational efficiency and effectiveness.

(4) The application of manpower analysis in Malaysia had many weaknesses. It would have been more useful to examine not broad national aggregates but rather the employment and education needs of a few key industries. These could be industries where shortages of educated manpower were a problem, which were particularly important for national development, or which offered substantial employment opportunities. Or studies could investigate the need for specific occupations in short supply and with clear educational requirements (for example doctors or engineers). With such a change in orientation, manpower studies could explore directly the relationships between education, occupation, employment rates, productivity, and possibly skill substitution. The hypothesis that general education affects the amount and rate of on-job skill acquisition could be fruitfully investigated. One of the criticisms of manpower analysis is that it fails to take economic benefits into account, but it is entirely possible to combine quantitative assessment of demand for and output of various sorts of education—particularly the less-substitutable technical and professional specialties—with an examination of market factors.[36] If taken out of the realm of national-level analysis of "needs," manpower studies could overcome many of the theoretical and measurement problems criticized above and become more useful tools.

(5) Another modification of manpower analysis, incorporating qualitative as well as quantitative factors, would be changes in the direction of job analysis.[37] Job analysis, which is usually associated with administration and personnel management, involves detailed investigation of the tasks performed by various occupational groups and the skills and education needed to perform these tasks. Such information makes it possible to determine whether educational programs are or could be preparing graduates who are well suited for certain occupations. A form of job analysis could indicate, for example, whether the education of science majors or comprehensive school graduates actually equipped them better for certain occupations than academic graduates. Such information is rarely used in planning the content of education courses, although it is more frequently used in connection with specific trades training. It is detailed, costly, and time-consuming and requires expertise not usually available in developing countries. Broad-scale studies at the national level will probably always be infeasible, but investigation of a few important occupations and their educational needs, perhaps with international technical assistance, would be feasible and potentially useful. The utility of job analysis would be particularly great in planning vocational education programs.

(6) The question of internal or X-efficiency has received relatively little attention in this case study, although the data suggest

105

the existence of significant X-inefficiencies. Table 4.11 shows that expenditures per pupil do not appear to have significant impact upon an index of educational performance that measures the difference between classes' entering and leaving scores. Schools in the highest cost quartile have <u>lower</u> average performance than those in the middle two quartiles.

Turning the analysis around, as in Table 14.12, schools in the highest performance quartile exhibited per student costs almost

TABLE 4.11

Relationship Between Per-Pupil Expenditure
and Performance

Schools by per-pupil expenditure category	Index of educational performance	
	Malay medium	English medium
Highest cost quartile	7.62	7.87
Middle two quartiles	8.88	8.36
Lowest cost quartile	7.91	7.47

<u>Source</u>: Secondary School Survey data.

TABLE 4.12

Relationship Between Performance and
Per-Pupil Expenditure

Schools by performance category	Average performance index score		Average per-pupil expenditure	
	Malay	English	Malay	English
Highest performance quartile	11.69	11.10	246	302
Mean, all schools	8.31	8.00	247	301

<u>Source</u>: Secondary School Survey data.

identical to the mean costs in each medium. These indications that higher performance can be achieved without increases in costs suggest strongly that research on the internal effectiveness and efficiency of education can lead to savings in resources or improvements in performance within resource constraints. The issue of X-efficiency will be considered further in later chapters and in Appendix D.

NOTES

1. Malaysian Department of Statistics, Malaysian Socio-Economic Survey of Households, 1967-68. (Kuala Lumpur: 1971.) Preliminary data were available to researchers in 1969 and 1970.

2. O. D. Hoerr, 'Economic Growth Requirements for Education," unpublished memorandum to Thong Yaw Hong, Director of the Economic Planning Unit, and Mohd. Noor Hassan, Deputy Director; (Kuala Lumpur: September 20, 1969.) A later analysis of the same data by Hoerr appears in "Education, Income, and Equity in Malaysia," Economic Development and Cultural Change 21, no. 2 (January, 1973): 247-73.

3. Malaysian Department of Statistics (N. S. Choudry), Manpower Survey, 1965: States of Malaya, Technical Report (Kuala Lumpur: Department of Statistics, 1966).

4. H. S. Beebout, "EPRD Secondary School Survey: Preliminary Report," Education Planning and Research Division, 1971, Mimeographed.

5. H. S. Beebout, "The Production Surface for Academic Achievement: An Economic Study of Malaysian Secondary Education." Ph.D. dissertation, Department of Economics, University of Wisconsin at Madison, 1972.

6. R. H. Sheath and D. J. Vickery, "Secondary General School Buildings in Malaysia—Their Functions, Utilization and Costs," (Colombo: Asian Regional Institute for School Building Research, April, 1971), preliminary report. Mimeographed.

7. Lourdesamy, "The Vocational School Program in Malaysia: A Study in Effective Development Administration" Ph.D. dissertation, University of Pittsburgh, Graduate School of Public and International Affairs, 1972.

8. Tables from the computerized model are presented in Appendix C. The model showed pupil flows through the system from the entering (grade one) population through the first year of university education; teacher needs; and recurrent costs.

9. Data on capital costs per pupil place under various assumptions are from Vickery and Sheath, op. cit., p. 35.

10. Statement by the World Bank to the Government of Malaysia, cited in Education Planning in Economic Development: A Proposal for Malaysia, a report by George Tobias, Ford Foundation Program Advisor to the Minister of Education, Kuala Lumpur, 1968, p. 3.

11. Blaug, An Introduction to the Economics of Education (London: Allen Lane The Penguin Press, 1970), p. 224.

12. Hoerr, op. cit., p. 266. He notes (p. 260n) that the data on unemployment among recent graduates are "very unsatisfactory," but that their indications are still unmistakable.

13. Ibid., pp. 252-55. Hoerr acknowledges both these problems. His adjustment for multicolinearity seems arbitrary.

14. Government of Malaysia, Second Malaysia Plan: 1971-1975.

15. Ibid., p. 2.

16. Ibid., p. 231.

17. Beebout, "The Production Surface for Academic Achievement," op. cit., pp. 161-77. For a description of the longitudinal performance indicator, see Beebout, "EPRD Secondary School Survey: A Preliminary Report," op. cit., pp. 93-95. Measurement of such a longitudinal performance indicator is rare, even in the best of economic analyses of education. H. H. Thias and M. Carnoy note the absence of such data in Kenya in Cost Benefit Analysis in Education: A Case Study of Kenya, IBRD Staff Paper No. 14 (Baltimore: Johns Hopkins Press, 1972), pp. 143-44.

18. Beebout, "The Production Surface for Academic Achievement," op. cit., pp. 168-69.

19. Beebout, "The Production Surface for Academic Achievement," op. cit. p. 169.

20. Ibid.

21. See Blaug, op. cit., pp. 269-81 for an extended discussion of declining productivity in British secondary schools, the "folk-lore of the small class," and other indications that facilities, class size, and expenditures did not affect performance.

22. Second Malaysia Plan, op. cit., p. 234.

23. Beebout, "The Production Surface for Academic Achievement," op. cit., p. 118. This criterion produced a low estimate of science enrollment because many students who were enrolled in science courses chose not to be examined in these more difficult fields.

24. Ibid., Table V-1.

25. Beebout, "EPRD Secondary School Survey: A Preliminary Report," op. cit., p. 18.

26. Statement of Tuan Haji Hamdan bin Sheik Tahir, director general of education, to the National Seminar on Educational Planning, Kuala Lumpur: June, 1970.

27. See Hoerr, Economic Development and Cultural Change op. cit., p. 257.

28. Beebout, "The Production Surface for Academic Achievement, op. cit., p. 177.

29. Ibid.

30. For a description of how vocational and technical education developed in Malaysia, see I. Lourdesamy, op. cit., Chapter I.

31. Report of the Commission on Teachers' Salaries (The Aziz Commission), Kuala Lumpur: 1971, p. 223.

32. Educational Statistics of Malaysia (Kuala Lumpur: Dewan Bahasa dan Pustaka, 1970), p. 54.

33. Hoerr, op. cit., p. 257.

34. Blaug, op. cit., p. 27.

35. Beebout, "The Production Surface for Academic Achievement," op. cit., pp. 196-201.

36. See for example K. Arrow and W. M. Capron, "Dynamic Shortages and Price Rises; The Engineer-Scientist Case," Quarterly Journal of Economics 72, no. 2 (1959): 292-308. This theoretical study of market behavior with changing demand and of factors causing a lag in adjustment in supply is a far cry from manpower studies usually carried out in developing countries, but illustrates ways that economic factors can be related to quantitative measurement of requirements and output.

37. For a discussion of the necessity to perform job analysis in connection with meaningful manpower studies, see M. Blaug, op. cit., p. 156.

5

ANALYSIS OF THE
VOCATIONAL EDUCATION
ALTERNATIVE

The preceding chapter reviewed the interrelated decisions regarding access to the upper secondary level. The central decision that was taken was to permit a relatively liberal rate of access to Form IV, close to the 60 percent upper bound. The decision was taken despite the possibility that increased enrollment in academic upper secondary would tend to create over production of this category of school leavers, and decreases in their employment rates and income. Two alternative approaches to improving employability and earning power of academic graduates were then considered: shifting a portion of enrollment from the arts to the science stream, or establishing comprehensive education at the upper secondary level. This chapter considers a third alternative: expanding vocational school enrollment as a portion of total upper secondary enrollment. This, it was thought, would produce graduates who were prepared to enter skilled blue-collar occupations where employment opportunities were greater and income would be higher.

A major difficulty in analyzing the science and comprehensive alternatives was lack of data on their benefits. A longitudinal study of the employment and income experience of a cohort of vocational graduates permits more detailed analysis of vocational schools' effectiveness in this chapter. The aims of the chapter are as follows:

1. To illustrate further the way that high-level policy choices tend to break down into lower-level comparisons of the effectiveness of alternatives;

2. To illustrate the feasibility of gathering longitudinal, performance-related data and some of the uses of such data for policy analysis;

3. To demonstrate some applications of economic analysis—even in fairly unsophisticated forms—as a way of looking at policy choices; and

4. To indicate the importance of examining the internal effectiveness of education programs. A related issue concerns the role of program objectives in influencing program performance.

Vocational enrollment had always been small in Malaysia. Only a few hundred graduates were produced each year until the late nineteen sixties.[1] (See Appendix A for a description of the vocational education program.) The First Malaysia Plan (1965-1970) called for substantial expansion of the vocational stream. Changes were made in the nature of the vocational schools with the elimination of the former Rural Trade Schools (Sekolah Lanjutang Kampong) and enrollment grew from 553 in 1965 to 2,672 (in seven new vocational schools) in 1970. This still constituted only about 3 percent of total upper secondary enrollment. The World Bank concluded that many more vocational schools should be created and approved a loan to construct six additional schools in the First Malaysia Plan. (Due to various delays, these schools were not actually begun until the Second Malaysian Plan period.) On the basis of manpower estimates, the bank estimated that 13,000 vocational graduates would be needed annually from 1971 to 1975. This implied enrollment of 26,000 in the two-year course, or a ten fold increase above 1970 enrollment. The Higher Education Planning Committee (HEPC) also assumed that vocational education should be greatly expanded.[2] The climate of official opinion thus favored major expansion of the vocational stream.

There were at the same time some indications of problems with the vocational program. Unemployment among vocational graduates was mentioned and some employers expressed dissatisfaction with the quality of vocational preparation.[3] These warning signals were strongly denied by the Technical Division, the branch of the Ministry of Education responsible for vocational schools, but they indicated a need for specific policy research on the costs and effectiveness of the vocational program before making heavy investments in more of the same sort of schools.

The manpower study and interpretations placed upon its data indicated a need for expansion. Hoerr's rate-of-return analysis did not identify vocational graduates specifically, since they were very few in number. And since there had been a change in the nature of vocational education around 1965, it would have been impossible to obtain relevant long-term age-income profiles for graduates of the new schools in any event. A longitudinal survey of vocational graduates, conducted privately by I. Lourdesamy, thus came at an opportune time.[4] Although the idea of evaluative research on vocational graduates was opposed by the Technical Division, the EPRD lent its official support to the study, aided in obtaining and processing some of the data, and received copies of Lourdesamy's raw data in 1971.

111

Lourdesamy's principal interest in the vocational program was as a case study in development administration. His data, however, were drawn from a full survey of the first cohort of graduates from the new schools and were of broader interest. The survey covered all members of the first graduating class in 1969.* An 86 percent response was obtained, and tracing and follow-up checks on a group of nonrespondents indicated that no apparent biases existed between those who responded voluntarily and those who did not. For two of the seven schools, a more lengthy questionnaire covering more variables yielded information in greater depth. The survey was conducted in the last quarter of 1970. The 1969 graduates had completed their schooling some twelve months earlier but, because of delays in grading and returning their examinations, had not received their Malaysian Certificate of Vocational Education (MCVE) until late March or April of 1970. There is, therefore, some ambiguity about whether they had been in the labor market and seeking work for twelve months or only six. This factor was raised as a criticism of the study, as will be discussed below.

FINDINGS OF THE SURVEY
OF VOCATIONAL GRADUATES[†]

Employment

The most striking finding of the study of 1969 graduates was that 73 percent were unemployed! Criticisms of the study by the Technical Division stated that the graduates had been surveyed too soon after receiving their certificates, and that the findings were biased toward high unemployment rates because the boys had not

———————

*Graduates of the earlier vocational education program in 1968 were also surveyed, and data from this survey serve as a comparison with the data on the first group to graduate from the new vocational schools. Since the nature of the education offered was different in both name and practice, comparisons between the two groups require caution. For a description of the survey methodology, see Lourdesamy, "The Vocational School Program in Malaysia."[4] Chapter I, ca. pp. 35-52. Most references to this source will be by chapter, since the writer's early copy is unpaginated.

[†]The data presented below are based upon tabulation of Lourdesamy's raw data, which were made available to the Education Planning and Research Division and tabulated to the writer's specifications.

112

TABLE 5.1

1970 Employment of 1969 Vocational School Leavers
by Trade Course Taken
(in numbers and percent)

Course	Number		Percent	
	Employed	Unemployed	Employed	Unemployed
TV and radio	23	40	37	63
Building con- struction	39	209	16	84
Welding and sheet metal	35	104	25	75
Machine shop	59	110	35	65
Motor mechanics	54	145	27	73
Electrical in- stallation	61	117	34	66
All courses	271	725	29	71

Source: Tabulations of Vocational School Survey Data.

had time to find work.[5] While there may be some validity to this
charge, and employment rates might be expected to rise with the
passage of time, the unemployment rate seems egregiously high
for a time six months after graduates received their certificates
and twelve months after they left school. Table 5.1 shows the employment results by trade course pursued. While some trade courses
apparently led to higher employment rates, none of the rates could
be called satisfactory.

Investigation of the employment rates among the graduates
of the earlier type of trade schools (1968) revealed that 63 percent
were employed and 37 percent were not. Clearly more time in the
labor market led to higher employment rates, but a 37 percent unemployment rate after nearly two years in the labor market still
indicated that vocational graduates were not readily snapped up by
eager employers.

Comparative data on employment rates among nonvocational
upper secondary graduates were scarce and those that were available
had shortcomings. The Socio-Economic Survey data showed employment among males aged 15 to 19 who had completed 10 years of
schooling (that is, Form IV) to be 33 percent in 1967.[6] Other data
from a private market research survey indicated 28 percent unemployment among upper secondary graduates aged 15 to 20 in 1968.[7] The

113

ta are for five-year age ranges and the definitions of labor force
articipation and unemployment may differ, thus they cannot be considered precise measurements of relative unemployment rates. They
are, however, reasonably consistent with each other. The unemployment rates for all upper secondary graduates are high, as Hoerr
had indicated, but not as high as the rates for vocational graduates.

Table 5.2 shows the duration of employment among employed
vocational graduates. The data show that some of those employed
had found work immediately after leaving school (well before their
MCVE certificates were available). Most had been employed less
than six months. The number employed for less than three months
was less than those employed from three to six months, thus the
number finding work in each successive three-month period had
begun to decline. The last point indicates that finding work would
not become easier for the large portion of graduates still unemployed.

Income

The only income data available for vocational school graduates are the starting salaries earned by employed members of the
first cohort to enter the labor force. Table 5.3 shows the distribution
of starting salaries. The profile shows that, while a few graduates
received high starting salaries, most did not. Thirty-nine percent
of employed graduates received less than $100 per month (equivalent

TABLE 5.2

Duration of Employment for Employed
1969 Vocational School Graduates

Length of Time Employed	Number	Percent
Less than 3 months	80	30
3 to 6 months	104	38
6 to 9 months	51	19
9 to 12 months	24	9
12 to 15 months	12	4
Total	271	100

Source: Tabulations of Vocational School Survey Data.

114

TABLE 5.3

Levels of Starting Salaries of Employed
Vocational Graduates
(Malaysian Dollars)

Monthly Salary Range	Number of Graduates	Percent
$0 to $50	4	1.5
$50 less than $75	40	14.7
$75 less than $100	62	22.8
$100 less than $125	64	23.5
$125 less than $150	48	17.7
$150 less than $175	29	10.7
$175 less than $200	10	3.7
$200 less than $300	8	2.9
Over $300	2	0.7
No response	5	1.8
Total	272	100.0

Source: Tabulations of Vocational School Survey Data.

TABLE 5.4

Average Monthly Earning of Employed
Graduates by Trade Course
(Malaysian Dollars)

Trade Course Taken	Average Monthly Earnings of Employed Graduates
Motor mechanics	106.02
Building construction	106.18
Sheet metal and Welding	109.77
Machine shop practice	120.09
T. V. and radio	127.73
Electricity	130.28

Source: Tabulations of Vocational School Survey Data.

.S. $33.00 per month). Most were grouped in the range from $75
$125. The average salary for all employed graduates was $116.

There were some differences between the average earnings of
graduates of different trade courses. Average earnings of the lowest-
paid trade course graduates (motor mechanics) were 82 percent as
high as those of the highest-paid (electricity). Table 5.4 shows the
averages by trade course.

A further comparison of the effectiveness of the several trade
courses can be made by multiplying the average salary of employed
graduates in each trade course by the probability of employment for
that course. The resulting average salaries for employed and unemployed graduates, or expected income values of each trade course
provide an index of effectiveness. Table 5.5 shows such an analysis.
The ranking of the courses by this index differs somewhat from rankings by either income or employment alone, although the top and
bottom three courses are the same in all cases. Employability and
earning power are both indicators of how the market appraises the
graduates of the different courses. The Spearman coefficient of
rank correlation between the income and employment rankings for
the six trade courses is 0.49, indicating significant agreement.
Income and employability effects thus tend to reinforce each other.
While the earnings of graduates of the highest-income trade course
exceeded those of the lowest-income course by a factor of 0.23, the
top-ranked course in terms of expected income value exceeds the
bottom-ranked course by a factor of 1.78. This analysis indicates

TABLE 5.5

Expected Income Value of Trade Courses
(Malaysian Dollars)

Trade Course	Average Monthly Earnings	Probability of Employment	Expected Income Value
Building construction	106	0.16	17.00
Sheet Metal and Welding	110	0.25	27.50
Motor mechanics	106	0.27	28.60
Machine shop practice	120	0.35	42.00
Electricity	130	0.34	42.20
T. V. & radio	128	0.37	47.36

Source: Calculated from Tables 5.7 and 5.4.

major differences in effectiveness between different sorts of vocational education and suggests various sorts of further research and analysis on internal effectiveness.

Information on starting salaries of nonvocational school leavers at the Form V level are scarce, as noted in Chapter 4. The data cited in Chapter 4 indicated starting salaries ranging from $160 to $250 per month.[8] If these data can be relied upon at all, they indicate a marked disparity between vocational and academic graduates' starting salaries.

If one examines the frequency distribution of employed vocational graduates' starting salaries in comparison with Lee's $160 to $250 range, the disparity is made more clear. Figure 5.1 shows this relationship.

FIGURE 5.1

Starting Salary Indicators:
Frequency Distribution of Vocational Graduates;
Range of Nonvocational Graduates

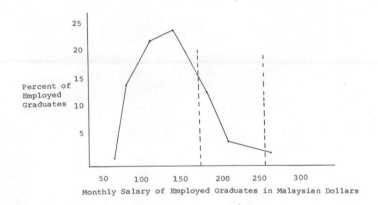

Monthly Salary of Employed Graduates in Malaysian Dollars

———— Actual distribution of employed vocational graduates

------ Indicated range of starting salaries of employed non-vocational graduates; data are from E. Lee and presumably indicate a range one standard deviation above and below the mean

117

Relevance of Vocational Education to Employment

Employed graduates were asked to indicate their present job. The researcher, Lourdesamy, then identified each job as either "technical" or "nontechnical." Graduates were also asked to state their opinion regarding whether their vocational education was relevant to their present job. Table 5.6 shows the responses to these two questions. While three-fourths of those who had found work reported that it was technical in nature, a lower proportion reported that their education was related to their job. Thus if the criterion of success for vocational education were employment in an occupation for which the education is relevant, the success rate would be only about 16 percent (27 percent employment x 56 percent in related jobs).

Quality of Vocational Graduates

Lourdesamy also obtained qualitative impressions of the performance of vocational graduates on the job from interviews with 19 employers of vocational graduates. "Data obtained on the perceptions

TABLE 5.6

Relationship of Training to Employment Among
Employed 1969 Vocational School
Graduates

Technical or Non-technical Job	Number	Percent
Technical	206	76
Nontechnical	64	23
Not clear	2	1
No response	0	0
Total	272	100
Relationship of job to education:		
Related	151	56
Not related	116	42
No response	5	2
Total	272	100

Source: Tabulations of Vocational School Survey Data.

TABLE 5.7

Employers Perceptions of Quality of
Vocational Graduates

	Good	Perceptions of Quality Satisfactory	Poor	Total
Number of employers	2	4	13	19
Percent	11	21	68	100

Source: Lourdesamy, "The Vocational School Program in Malaysia," op. cit., Chapter III.

of employers of vocational school graduates seem also to indicate that the vocational schools are producing low level skills. In the course of the interviews, employers of vocational graduates were asked their perceptions of the "quality" (level of skill) of the graduates."[9] Table 5.7 shows Lourdesamy's tabulations of their responses (good, satisfactory, or poor).

Response to a questionnaire item directed to unemployed vocational graduates indicated that 42 percent attributed their inability to find jobs to "poor quality of the vocational school program."[10] Direct interviews with employed graduates revealed complaints about lack of "practical work," poor workship facilities, and inadequate teaching at their former vocational schools. Thus both employers and graduates perceived the quality of preparation provided by the vocational schools as unsatisfactory.

Criticisms of the Data and Research Methodology

Defenders of the existing vocational education program raised a number of objections to the longitudinal study, arguing that its results were biased toward high unemployment.[11] These criticisms are reviewed below:

1. The survey was conducted too soon after the boys received their MCVE certificates, therefore they had not had sufficient time to find work.

A single survey conducted 6 months after the certificates were received and 12 months after the boys left school can perhaps be criticized on the basis of timing. But since the 1969 cohort was the first to graduate from the new-type schools, there was no earlier comparable group to study. The problems revealed are so glaring, that, despite possible validity to this criticism, surveying the boys after 18 or 24 months in the labor market would probably not have produced data indicating other policy conclusions. Data on the duration of employment (Table 5.2 above) indicate that some boys found work immediately after leaving school, without their certificates. Other data from the in-depth questionnaires reveal that most had sought work and considered themselves unemployed for a full 12 months. As noted in Chapter 3, there are trade-offs between timeliness of data and completeness. In this case, waiting for more complete data would probably not have changed many of the findings (for example, on salary levels, relevance, employers' perceptions, and so on).

2. Performance of the first cohort of graduates was not representative of what the program would accomplish later because the first cohort to enter the vocational schools had been poor students.

Representatives of the Technical Division presented data indicating that the grade averages of later entering classes were higher than earlier groups and argued that the first (surveyed) cohort was therefore a poor example. The vocational schools had traditionally been considered a last resort for gaining access to upper secondary. The fact that increasing numbers of "A" candidates elected to enter vocational schools in subsequent years might have been significant. But data from the subset of in-depth questionnaires reveal no significant relationship (or, if anything, a negative relationship) between the graduates' LCE (entering) grade and subsequent employment rates. Nor are there significant relationships between grades of those who sat for the London City and Guilds examination (taken upon completing Form V) and employment rates. Table 5.8 shows these relationships. The argument that the surveyed cohort's low employment rates were unrepresentative due to low academic standards thus looses some of its force.

3. The wording of the covering letter sent with the questionnaires may have biased responses, since it implied that employment assistance might be offered to those who responded that they were unemployed.

Lourdesamy's study was called a "Follow-Up Study to Help Vocational School Pupils." He acknowledges that this title and the phraseology of the covering letter might have tended to elicit higher response rates from unemployed graduates, or to induce employed graduates to say they were unemployed in the hope of getting information on better jobs. But a "tracking" exercise, in which some nonrespondents from each school were traced and interviewed personally, indicated no apparent differences between their employment rates and those of voluntary respondents.[12] The criticism of bias seems unjustified.

TABLE 5.8

Comparisons of LCE (entering) and City and Guilds Grades and Employment Ratios (in percent)

LCE Grade	Employment Rate	City and Guilds Grade	Employment Rate
A	21	Credit	38
B	21	Pass	25
C	32	Fail	33

Source: Tabulations of subsets of questionnaires: in-depth questionnaires, and questionnaires of boys who sat for the London City and Guilds exam.

There were other criticisms raised by the Technical Division, which claimed that there were differences between the longer in-depth questionnaire (used for graduates of two schools) and the main questionnaire. The questions concerning employment and income did not, however, differ between the two questionnaires. Use of different questionnaires was occasioned by discovery, during the survey, that data on more variables would be desirable. While not a preferred research practice, expanding the questionnaires was unlikely to have altered the findings on the questions common to both. The main finding of the survey, in the context of this case, was that vocational education did not lead to higher rates of employment and income among its graduates than alternative forms of upper secondary education. The criticisms of the methodology do not impugn the validity of this finding.

AN ASSESSMENT OF VOCATIONAL EDUCATION AS AN ALTERNATIVE INVESTMENT

The data on performance of vocational graduates in the labor market revealed such serious problems in absolute terms that comparison of this alternative with those considered in Chapter 4 need not be elaborate. The data indicate that vocational graduates experienced higher unemployment and earned lower starting salaries than nonvocational graduates. Many of those employed were working in nontechnical positions or in occupations to which their specific trades training was not related. A high proportion of interviews with employers of vocational graduates indicated that the preparation of vocational graduates they employed had been poor. Some trades specialties such as machine shop practice, electricity, and T.V. and radio produced higher average incomes (of employed plus unemployed graduates) than others such as building construction. This suggested that enrollment might be shifted from the least successful specialties to those with higher pay-offs. But not even the best specialties compared favorably with nonvocational education in terms of employment and income.*

On the cost side, vocational education was considerably more expensive than academic education, due to higher capital costs for specialized workshops, higher-paid specialist teachers, expendable materials costs, and so on. Cost data were again very scarce; data from the Technical Division showed much lower costs than those from other sources. Average costs per pupil varied widely during the first years in which the new schools were operated (due to changes in utilization rates) but exhibited a clear downward trend as enrollment approached capacity. Data from the EPRD for 1967 indicated capital costs per pupil of $180 and recurrent costs of $660. Estimates from the Expenditure Budget for 1971 showed annual recurrent expenditures per vocational pupil declining from $570 in 1969 to $548 in 1970 and an estimated $499 in 1971.[13] The Technical Division claimed recurrent costs were on the order of $400 per pupil per year, apparently based on 100 percent utilization of facilities. If one assumes less optimistic utilization rates, somewhat higher than in 1971 but less than 100 percent, an estimate of $470 in recurrent costs per pupil seems reasonable. Another rough but reasonable estimate of $150 in capital costs per pupil year brings the total cost of vocational education to $620.[†] This represents a total cost increment over academic upper secondary education of $350 per year or $700 for the two-year cycle, which is slightly lower than the cost of the comprehensive school alternative.

In present value terms, the cumulative cost of producing a vocational graduate would be $9,305 or an 8.5 percent increase over

_____

*Multiplying the low point of the nonvocational salary range calculated by Eddy Lee ($160) by the unemployment rate for unemployed graduates from the Socio-Economic Survey (33 percent) yields a minimum expected income value for nonvocational graduates of $52.80. This is 11 percent higher than the best vocational trade course.

†These approximate figures do not provide insight into possible cost differences between trade specialties. As in the case of the other alternatives, cost data are far from adequate.

the comparable cumulative cost of an academic Form V school leaver.
Following the argument of the previous chapter, this would imply
that the present value of the lifetime benefit stream of vocational
graduates would have to be $9,305 or more in order to make the
investment at least as attractive as academic upper secondary; and,
by way of several strong assumptions regarding the similarity of
the two age-income profiles, further implies that average starting
salaries should be about 8.5 percent higher than those of nonvocational
graduates. The data on starting salaries of the first cohort of vocational graduates indicate clearly that this was not, in fact, the case.
Average starting salaries, adjusted for employment rates, were
lower for vocational graduates than for the graduates of the academic
upper secondary stream.

It gives one pause to realize that expansion of the vocational
stream, indeed a very large expansion, was a highly advocated approach to "meeting the nation's manpower needs" and solving the
problem of overproduction of academic graduates. Even a relatively
straightforward piece of policy research (requiring one man-year
of effort) produced data indicating that the existing form of vocational
education had serious shortcomings. If this aspect of the case study
does nothing else, it illustrates the utility of examining the performance
of specific programs, preferably in comparison with other alternatives,
before making higher-level decisions based upon aggregate indicators
of manpower needs !

Other policy conclusions emerged from the study that have not
been emphasized in the analysis of employment and income. One of
the points that Lourdesamy raises in his analysis of the data from
an administrative standpoint is that the vocational program made very
little use of what he calls "linkage institutions"—public employment
services and job counselling agencies that could have aided the boys
in finding work. Other information on the content of vocational courses,
based on examination of the curriculum, visits to the schools, and
questioning employers on their needs, indicated that internal changes
could have improved the graduates' ability to find jobs and earn more.
Boys who lived more than ten miles from a large town had significantly
lower employment rates than those who lived closer to urban job
sites, suggesting that efforts to aid the rural boys in their job searches
and provide better employment information might have had an impact
on employment rates and overall program effectiveness. If the objective of vocational education is to equip its graduates for skilled
occupations and improve their employability, then the problems
that Lourdesamy found are indicative of "X-inefficiency." If more
efforts to aid graduates in finding employment could have increased
their employment rates even marginally, then the effectiveness of
the program in comparison with other alternatives could have been

increased. The same applies to changes in the course offerings that might have affected graduates' earning power.

This raises another important point: perception of the objectives of the vocational program by its administrators. Chapter 2 discussed the need to clarify program objectives as part of an economic or systems analysis way of looking at problems. The Technical Division, which controlled the vocational program, did not consider that it was responsible for helping its graduates to find employment. The writer heard many statements to this effect and Lourdesamy documents still others.[14] An artificial distinction between "vocational education" and "vocational training" became a focus of attention in planning meetings, with the Technical Division maintaining that its function was "education," and that it was not concerned with whether graduates found jobs. Yet vocational upper secondary education was a terminal cycle, that is, its graduates could do nothing else but enter the labor market. Its course content was clearly trades-oriented and the justification for expanding the vocational stream was to meet manpower needs. The Technical Division's objectives extended no farther than the schools' walls, however, and it rejected the findings of the survey.* It was suboptimizing, but in a noneconomic way. The need for decision makers and analysts to examine specific program objectives and determine whether they are compatible with higher-level objectives (and whether program managers perceive the objectives in ways that do not conflict with higher-level perceptions) is thus illustrated. The simplest sort of policy analysis, applied at the micro level, can illuminate these questions.

What of the decisions that were actually taken? At least vocational education did not become the focus of a major investment effort, as it might have if only manpower information had been considered. The six additional vocational schools that had originally been scheduled for the First Malaysia Plan were continued as investment projects in the Second Malaysia Plan, perhaps out of inertia and a sense of commitment to go through with these internationally-funded projects. The Technical Division, still claiming that it was providing "vocational education," undertook no revision of its existing program to the writer's knowledge. (Rather than consider reducing enrollment in the least effective trade specialty, building construction, the Technical Division recommended legislation to require contractors

---

*Readers interested in administrative aspects of the case are referred to Lourdesamy, op. cit. Possible reasons for objections to evaluation and resistance to considering alternatives are suggested in E. E. Hagen, "Some Cultural and Personality Factors in Economic Development," Development Digest, 3, no. 2 (July, 1965): 46-59.

to hire graduates of this stream !) While the lack of response to the survey data does nothing to indicate the efficacy of analysis, even when the findings are quite clear, it does not deny the importance of such research. Perhaps the availability of the information will lead to future moves to improve the employability and earning power of vocational graduates. The need to create not only the analytical capability to conduct such research but also an ability on the part of decision makers to absorb and use its findings is also strongly suggested, as will be discussed in the final chapter.

The vocational education portion of the total case study does not indicate what course of action is absolutely best. It is not clear that any analytical approach could do this, although combinations of internal effectiveness analysis and standard applications of rate-of-return analysis could probably provide a fairly clear guide for action. The analysis presented here focuses upon the relative merits of a limited set of alternatives. In this sense, it indicates that vocational education is not a preferred investment in comparison with academic upper secondary education. This is not to say that academic upper secondary is necessarily a "good" investment in itself. The problems of overproduction of academic upper secondary graduates remain. Lack of information on the benefits of the science or comprehensive education alternatives precludes clear conclusions on the desirability of investing in them. The information and analysis presented above simply indicate that, if implementation of these alternatives could produce moderate improvements in employability and income, on the order of 3 to 10 percent above the experience of purely academic graduates, they would be worth exploring further. The focus of the analysis is thus not upon what is best in absolute terms but, within the given context, which of several alternatives are better than others.

From the standpoint of the objectives of this chapter, the vocational case accomplishes several things. It illustrates the feasibility of gathering policy-relevant data that meet some of the criteria set forth in Chapter 3. It further illustrates some simple analytic uses to which such information can be put to improve the functioning of the system (even though the decisions actually taken were not especially responsive to the information). And it indicates the need to carry out the fundamental steps of economic analysis discussed in Chapter 2—clarifying objectives, comparing alternatives, and measuring the performance and costs of each—before undertaking major educational investments.

CRITICISMS OF THE CASE

The case is far from an ideal example of how economic analysis can be applied to lower-level policy choices. The following points are probably a minimal set of criticisms.

1. The case does not illustrate a clear, straightforward systems anslysis, in which objectives, alternatives, cost and benefit data, and elegant analytical models are brought together to indicate preferred courses of action.

2. The conclusions that do emerge from the piecemeal analyses are not very clear.

3. There are few indications that policies actually adopted proceeded from the analysis.

4. Much of the limited structure that appears in the case has been introduced by the writer after the fact.

5. While some of the data are unusually good, others are rough and approximate.

6. The methodological tools applied are either very simple (as in the case of basic cross tabulations), very crude, or even of questionable validity (the backward benefit-cost approach).

7. Many important aspects of the case have been inadequately explored.

As noted at the outset, if many ideal examples existed, the arguments of this study would be unnecessary.* Despite its inadequacies, the case does provide an illustration of many of the points raised in earlier chapters, including both the negative points regarding the standard planning approaches and more positive indications of what might be done to improve upon them. The policy questions addressed are real (and likely to arise in other developing countries). The very inadequacy and inconclusiveness of the case may illustrate the need for a continuous approach to policy research and analysis: the need to generate new alternatives, gather additional data, and perform more refined studies is apparent.

The failure of decision makers to act on the basis of evidence is at least partly because not all the information presented here was available at the time. Nor was the available information marshalled very effectively to influence decisions. There is a need for administrators to learn how to understand and use analysis, just as there

---

*Professor Roland McKean has invoked the "Cub Scout" theorem of systems analysis in situations where analytical tools can provide only imperfect policy guidance: "We do our best."

is a need to develop analytical capability in the planning office. And, of course, administrators are moved by many influences, of which planning is rarely the most important.

In terms of the limited objectives stated at the beginning of Chapters 4 and 5, the case can be considered reasonably successful. From the writer's standpoint, if it serves to raise questions about the standard planning approaches that are so widely taught and applied, and to suggest that another orientation to planning and analysis might be more fruitful, it has served its purpose.

NOTES

1. I. Lourdesamy, "The Vocational School Program in Malaysia." Ph.D. dissertation, University of Pittsburgh, 1972.

2. Report of the Higher Education Planning Committee (Kuala Lumpur: 1967), p. 60. Mimeographed.

3. For example, see a statement by Dato Mohamed Yusof bin Haji Ahmad, executive secretary of the Malaysian Manufacturers Association, in the Straits Times, July 11, 1970, to the effect that vocational graduates were not prepared for "real-life conditions" in Malaysian factories.

4. Lourdesamy, op. cit.

5. Ibid. Chapter I.

6. Cited in Hoerr, "Education, Income and Equity in Malaysia," Economic Development and Cultural Change, 21, no. 2 (January, 1973).

7. Survey Research Malaysia, Kuala Lumpur: "SRM/Ford Social and Economic Survey (West Malaysia/1968)." This was a special tabulation, funded by the Ford Foundation, of data from a market research survey of 6,696 households in West Malaysia, weighted and expanded to represent the total population. The survey and analysis were of high quality. Reliability of data on smaller "cells" such as upper secondary graduates aged 15 to 20 was, however, subject to qualification.

8. Lee, Educational Planning In West Malaysia, op. cit.

9. Lourdesamy, op. cit., Chapter III.

10. Ibid.

11. Lourdesamy reviews the major criticisms and defends his methodology, op. cit., ca. pp. 44-45.

12. Ibid., Chapter I, ca. p. 50.

13. The Expenditure Budget of the Federal Government, 1971 (Kuala Lumpur: The Treasury, 1971), p. 421.

14. Lourdesamy, op. cit., Chapter I.

CHAPTER

6

CONCLUSIONS

THE PURPOSE AND ACCOMPLISHMENTS
OF THE STUDY

The preceding chapters have attempted to set forth a view of educational expenditure analysis that differs from the usual approaches to education sector planning. The study's intended contribution is not in theory or methodology but rather in the areas of the orientation and application of economic analysis to educational choices. The major conclusions that emerge regarding the practice of educational planning in developing countries are, I believe, important.

1. There is a hierarchy of educational expenditure decisions and the standard approaches to educational planning—rate-of-return and manpower analyses—provide information on only a limited range on this hierarchy, generally at a fairly high level of optimization.

2. Decisions at higher levels on the hierarchy are intimately related to lower-level decisions affecting the content, costs, and efficiency of different types of education.

3. The standard planning approaches produce information on a limited set of variables—far less than the full range of information that decision makers need.

4. The concept of X-efficiency, thus far explored mainly in the private industrial sector, is relevant to the education sector as well. If there are X-inefficiencies in education (that is, kinds of education operating below their efficient production possibility frontier), and there are indications that they do exist, then micro-analyses of the efficiency of educational projects in accomplishing their objectives are needed.

5. The major planning approaches address only questions of allocative efficiency on the assumption that productive units are

operating on their efficient possibility frontiers—even though available data strongly suggest that they are not.

6. Educational planning has lagged far behind the state of the art in other sectors. This is due in part to a preoccupation with the major planning approaches and in part to lack of data that would permit micro-analysis.

7. A changed orientation of educational planning is desirable for all these reasons. Such a modified approach to educational planning would approximate systems analysis. It would apply the known tools of economic analysis—especially benefit-cost and cost-effectiveness analysis, but also other forms of policy research—to choices at all levels of the decision hierarchy. The principal elements of such an approach are clarification of proximate program objectives, search for alternatives, compilation of data on program performance and costs, and comparison of alternative programs or policies in terms of analytical models. The models themselves can be very simple and still provide useful information for decision makers.

8. The data usually available in Ministries of Education in developing countries are not adequate for the sorts of analysis advocated. Suitable (micro-positive) data should be policy-relevant, disaggregated to the unit of analysis, and related to the costs and, most importantly, the performance of educational programs. It is possible to gather such data in developing countries at a reasonable cost.

Despite a generally critical tone toward the major educational planning approaches, it is not argued here that they are wrong at their foundations, but rather that their policy outputs are limited at best and their usual applications have many shortcomings. The major approaches can be modified and incorporated in an expanded conceptual framework for educational planning that will be more useful for policy guidance.

Such an expanded and reoriented conceptual framework fits the definition of educational planning offered in Chapter 1. It is a continuous process of gathering information and applying the most appropriate analytical tools available in order to provide evaluative information on the performance of educational programs, their efficiency, and ways in which they can be made to function better. Economists have tended to "plan from the top down" in terms of allocating resources between existing educational programs. Educational administrators, on the other hand, have not found such plans particularly useful. Neither group has fully perceived the need to bridge the gap between them, nor the potential utility of following the basic steps of systems analysis.

It is not argued that it is easy to apply systems analysis techniques to educational choices. On the contrary, there are many limitations on what can be accomplished in terms of providing better policy information. Given the nature of the educational process, the problems of measuring educational effectiveness, and the general scarcity of relevant data, there are limits on the usefulness of economic science in the education sector. But there is a useful domain within which economic analysis can improve the quality of educational decisions. It is possible to do a great deal more within this useful domain than has been done in the past. Generating better data that cast light upon significant policy questions is an important aspect of improving the quality of planning. Changing the orientation of educational expenditure analysis away from high-level allocative choices and toward the frequent and significant internal questions of program efficiency and effectiveness can bring the power of economic tools to bear upon a different set of questions. And answering these lower-level questions can have an important effect on the over all effectiveness of the sector.

The case study chapters illustrate various points made abstractly in earlier portions of this volume. Despite its limitations, the case study demonstrates that high-level choices break down into lower ones; that choices such as the access decision (a high-level, allocative choice) depend in part on the content of the education offered; that it is feasible to generate some data for the sort of analysis advocated here, and that suboptimizing analyses can cast light on choices between alternatives.

THE IMPORTANCE OF AN ALTERED
ORIENTATION OF PLANNING

A great deal of time and effort have been expended on manpower and rate-of-return studies (and on the controversy between the two approaches). The Mediterranean Regional Project alone, a multi-country exercise in manpower planning, involved a very great investment. Whether these efforts, particularly some of the manpower planning studies, have been worthwhile, is at least subject to honest question. The question can probably never be answered definitively since we cannot measure the outputs of planning studies. Whatever the answer, it can hardly be denied that a mixture of high-level allocative approaches and lower-level evaluative analyses would have been a more cost-effective utilization of scarce analytical resources than concentration on only the standard approaches.

How important are the lower-level analyses advocated here in comparison with allocative efficiency gains? Appendix D explores the potential welfare gain from reallocating resources between different educational levels and produces a very rough estimate that reallocating educational investments in Malaysia would produce $1.8 million per year in added social benefits. The appendix further considers a few partial indicators of potential X-efficiency improvements at the lower and upper secondary levels (which constitute less than 20 percent of the education budget). One change alone—increasing average class size by one pupil in the English medium, where class size appears to have no effect on academic performance—would produce a cost saving of $1.0 million. The costs of the highest-cost quartile of schools greatly exceeded that of the middle two cost quartiles, even though performance scores were the same. Eliminating the excess costs of the high-cost schools would produce a saving of $1.6 million. Other changes, still limited to the secondary level, include taking advantage of economies of scale ($0.46 million), and reduction of hostel places by 1,000 ($0.27 million). Other substantial X-efficiency improvements are indicated but we do not have adequate data to indicate their magnitudes. If similar cost reductions could be effected for primary and university education and in general administrative costs, the total X-efficiency gain would far exceed the benefits from equalizing returns to investments.

Another indication of the importance of the sort of analysis demonstrated in Chapters 4 and 5 is found by considering the policy conclusions that might have been reached on the basis of different sorts of planning approaches and information inputs.

Table 6.1 shows different policy conclusions regarding the desirable levels of upper secondary academic and vocational enrollment that would be indicated by different inputs of policy information. If policy makers relied only on the quantitative projection approach to planning or on the superficial findings of rate-of-return analysis, the information would lead them to choose high levels of upper secondary enrollment. Using the manpower approach in the way it was applied in Malaysia would suggest much lower enrollment in academic upper secondary and a major increase in vocational enrollment. Adding other bits of information in combination with the standard approaches would lead to significant modifications in the logical policy conclusions. The other bits of information considered here include the data on unemployment used by Hoerr to augment his rate of return findings, the equity information discussed in Chapter 4, and the information on comparison of alternatives that was developed in Chapters 4 and 5. By way of comparison, the conclusions actually reached and incorporated in the Second Malaysia Plan (SMP) are shown in the bottom line of the table.

This exercise in second-guessing what policy makers would do if presented with different information inputs is not a proof of the

TABLE 6.1

Variation in Policy Conclusions on Academic and Vocational Enrollment
Targets in Malaysia Based on Different Planning Approaches and Information Inputs

Planning Approaches And Information Inputs	Total Upper Secondary Enrollment[a]	Rational Policy Choices Implied	
		Vocational School Enrollment[b]	Would the Information Suggest Seeking Alternatives?
1. Quantitative projections approach	144,000	3,000	No
2. Manpower approach alone	120,000-	26,000	No
3. Rate-of-return approach alone	144,000	no information	No
4. Rate of return plus data on unemployment of secondary graduates	120,000+	4,200+	Possibly
5. Combination of 2 and 4	120,000	5,000+	Possibly
6. Combination of 5 plus equity information	140,000	5,000+	Possibly
7. Combination of 6 plus explicit comparison of alternatives	140,000	2,600-	Definitely
8. Choices incorporated in the SMP	140,000	4,200	Partially

[a]Based upon the flow model plus other known information. 120,000 assumes 50 percent access; 144,000 assumes 60 percent access; 140,000 is the level chosen in the SMP.

[b]Vocational enrollment of 2,600 was the level in 1970-71; 4,200 was the enrollment planned in the SMP; 26,000 was the assumed need based upon manpower analysis.

importance of a modified planning approach. It does, however, suggest that there are important differences in the policies chosen by rational decision makers on the basis of different kinds of information. The right-hand column considers whether planners would be led by the information to consider other educational alternatives, which is an extremely important effect of information.

Perhaps the most important effect of a changed orientation toward educational expenditure analysis would be its impact on educational innovations and change. Frederick Harbison is not alone in his feeling that, in many developing countries, "There is obvious over investment in the wrong kinds of education."[1] Educators and economists have tended to assume that existing forms of education are "all there are" and that they are operating on an efficient production possibility frontier. Given these assumptions, there is virtually no impetus to examine objectives, explore alternatives, and develop new ways for education systems in developing countries to contribute to social and economic change. It is not surprising, therefore, that education systems are operating in virtually the same fashion that they have for decades.* Concerned educators, economists, planners, and analysts have an obligation to seek alternative ways in which the heavy investments in education can have greater positive impact on socio-economic development. Such a search for alternatives requires a systems-oriented analytical framework and eclectic use of the available tools of analysis. It requires experimentation and sound policy research to evaluate the results of the experiments. It requires "feedback" of policy-relevant information to administrators on what works, what doesn't, and what internal changes in various kinds of education might increase their cost-effectiveness. In other sectors in the developing and developed world, such an approach to policy-making is taken for granted. Adaptation of systems analysis techniques to the education sector, with all its particular problems, will not be easily accomplished. But it is important to recognize the need to alter and improve the framework for analysis and planning.

THE PROBLEM OF STRATEGY SELECTION

The use of economic analysis to illuminate specific educational program choices does not fit the mold of "top down" planning. The

---

*The spate of interest in "educational technology" has thus far produced new ways of doing the same things; often at high cost. Breakthroughs, if they are to come, will probably occur not in "hardware" but in the fields of learning theory, the relationship between educational

partial bits of information that emerge from micro-analytical studies do not indicate clearly what grand strategy of education should be followed. While this criticism has some validity, there are several arguments that can be made in support of the sort of planning advocated in the previous chapters.

Use of economic analysis at low levels of optimization may be the best that is possible under the circumstances. The planning approaches that purport to offer definitive strategy guidance have serious weaknesses and blind spots. Moreover they are constrained to recommending strategic choices from among the available set of educational programs. Blaug seems to feel that the search for a perfect model is fruitless:

> It is high time that educational planning faced up squarely to the utter inability to foresee the consequences of big, lumpy decisions. Rational planning can never be much more than what Popper has called "piecemeal social engineering" and the maxim of educational planning should be "avoid binding commitments."[2]

While this comment is true as far as it goes, and provides support for a suboptimizing approach to planning, there is a bit more that can be said regarding the role of planning in shaping a strategy of educational development.

It was argued in Chapter 1 that educational planning serves as a source of "feedback" in a cybernetic process. In such a process, a system is guided by information from the environment and makes marginal adjustments to keep itself on course. Educational systems are not planned from some zero state at each decision-making juncture but rather modified at their margins. A micro-analytical approach to planning is compatible with the way choices are actually made. A cybernetic system does not proceed on the basis of a preconceived strategy but discovers and "learns" its way toward its goal on the basis of continuing information.* Evaluation of educational programs

---

inputs and academic performance, and in ways that the cognitive and socialization effects of education can contribute more effectively to achievement of socio-economic success.

*Clay Whithead discusses the distinction between "Cook's Tour" planning, which specifies each component of a strategy in advance, and "Lewis and Clark" planning, in which "the goal is far removed from near term activities and proximate goals must be derived as the operation evolves and learns about its environment." The former is what Lindblom and others have criticized as

in developing countries in terms of their contributions to national goals (or suboptimal goals, for that matter) has been seriously neglected. The concept of educational planning advanced in this study provides continuous evaluative information that permits an adaptive, evolving strategy to be developed. For various reasons discussed in Chapter 2, manpower and rate-of-return analysis are not well suited to providing continuous information on the performance of subsector programs. In other words, suboptimizing analyses of education programs, based on different kinds of data than those usually available, may be a more realistic approach to strategy formulation than any other.

If we accept Blaug's injunction to "avoid binding commitments," then an evolutionary approach to strategy formulation has other advantages: it considers particular problems as they arise, provides continuing information on how programs are performing, and is more sensitive to the need to adjust strategy than rational-comprehensive approaches. And there may be psychological advantages if educational administrators remain on a tentative footing and seek constant feedback on whether earlier commitments should be changed.

Continuous evaluation of education programs implies knowledge of the goals by which performance is evaluated. A cybernetic system is guided by feedback on how well it is proceeding toward its goal. As discussed in Chapter 2, it is often difficult to establish educational goals that are operationally meaningful. An important aspect of a systems approach to educational planning is the attempt to clarify program goals. Rational-comprehensive strategy making attempts to optimize in terms of highest level goals. The useful domain of economic analysis, however, is at lower levels on the hierarchy of optimization, where goals are more clear and less likely to be mutliple. In Chapter 5 we saw administrators, pursuing one goal (provision of vocationally prepared manpower), fail to perceive the importance of assuring that vocational graduates found employment. Clarity of goals and their interrelationships would preclude such wasteful confusion.

If goals are made explicit, then disjointed analysis and goal-oriented decision-making can achieve the kind of coherence sought by "top-down" planning approaches. The approach to planning advocated in the previous chapters can provide more information on goal accomplishment, and thus better guidance for strategy formulation, than high-level optimizing or rational-comprehensive planning.

---

rational-comprehensive planning. The latter, adaptive approach is what is suggested here for planning educational systems.

A related point concerns the search for alternatives and the need to conduct and evaluate experiments. Alternative search is another key aspect of a systems approach to educational planning in developing countries. The case study incorporated a comparison of alternatives. The situation in Malaysia was unusual in that there were several alternatives on which data for analysis could be gathered. Even so, it was clear that the alternatives considered were not enough, and that other approaches to increasing the employability and earning power of upper secondary graduates needed to be considered. Identification and selection of alternatives and design of sound evaluative schemes are almost unknown in the education sector in the developing world. The practice is not easy, as attempts to conduct major educational experiments in the United States have proved.3 But if we are to evolve more effective strategies for educational development, it will be necessary to seek alternatives, perform experiments, and conduct sound policy research on their results. The framework for analyzing educational expenditures is oriented toward these tasks.

IMPLICATIONS FOR TECHNICAL ASSISTANCE AND TRAINING IN EDUCATIONAL PLANNING

If we accept that a systems analysis framework for educational planning represents an improvement over the past state of the art, how can developing countries create the capability to carry on such planning? And how should international agencies and foundations that wish to aid in developing the capability for planning proceed with their efforts? There are several implications of this study that bear upon these questions.

The Concept of Planning. It would be well if the several parties concerned with educational planning—top educational administrators, planners themselves, and agencies providing technical assistance— perceived educational planning in the same way. Hopefully this study has succeeded in illustrating that planning should not be a straight-line process limited to preparation of medium-term plan documents, nor a source of "right" answers to high-level policy questions, but rather a continuous process that fits the definition offered in Chapter 1. If planning is viewed as a source of policy feedback on how the education system is functioning and how it can be improved, it can serve a more powerful role in shaping evolving educational strategies.

The Relationship between Planning and Administration. If the purpose of planning is to provide information for decision makers, then the link between planning and administration must be a close one. There

are various organizational arrangements by which the two can be
linked formally. None is particularly effective unless there are
meaningful channels of formal and informal communication and a
feeling of confidence on the part of administrators in the outputs of
planning. In the writer's experience, the task of developing an educational planning capability involves not only establishing a technically
competent planning group but also encouraging an understanding on
the part of administrators of how planning can serve them. For the
most part, planning offices must earn the confidence of administrators
by providing useful information. This task is easier if the orientation
of planning is toward policy questions with which administrators deal
frequently and on which they need information. In short, the link
between planning and administration is important and the conceptual
framework proposed here makes it easier to establish such a link.

The Relationship between Planning and Budgeting. The link between
planning and administration should include a link with the budget
office. Planning as conceived here is essentially a process of analyzing educational expenditure decisions. The close relationship
between systems analysis and program budgeting was discussed in
Chapter 2. It is surprising how frequently the planning and budgeting
functions are separated. Such separation works to the disadvantage
of both. The organizational relationship between planning and budgeting
is less important than free, two-way flows of information, both formally and informally. There are many forces that tend to pull planners
and budget specialists apart (one group is usually asking for more
money while the other is often forced to say "no"). But a shared
interest in efficiency and effectiveness and a shared need for information should act to draw them together.

Staffing Educational Planning Offices. Few Ministries of Education
in developing countries have adequately staffed planning groups. The
problems of getting, and keeping, an able cadre of planners are many
and a full discussion of them would lead beyond the present topic.
It is sufficient to say that planning groups should incorporate members
with varied skills. At least some members should have training and
experience that make it second nature to employ an economic choice
"way of looking at problems." This subject will be addressed further
in connection with training. Other members should have statistical
training that is relevant to policy research. Familiarity with sampling
techniques is important. Educators are usually in the majority so
there is little need to stress their involvement. Other specialties
such as educational sociology are highly desirable but may be drawn
into planning task forces from other sources as needed.

The Relationship between Planning and Research. The approach to planning advocated here depends heavily upon the provision of data that are relevant to policy issues. As indicated in Chapter 3, the sorts of data needed are rarely available, so planning groups should be capable of conducting frequent special studies. These differ from the sort of educational research that is usually conducted in universities. The research topics suggested in Chapter 3 give a flavor of the sorts of studies that are needed. Educational planning offices usually cannot and probably should not attempt to have a full complement of research personnel. (Given the ad hoc and problem-oriented nature of educational policy research, specialists might be needed in the area of curriculum evaluation at one time and in analysis of school construction costs shortly afterward.) Persons with special capabilities can be drawn from other offices and agencies as the needs arise. But the planning office should incorporate a capability to design policy studies and conduct its own research when necessary. The extension of the idea of educational planning to include research and evaluation is an important implication of this study.

The Choice of Subjects for Study. As emphasized in Chapter 3, the concept of cost-effectiveness should be applied to the use of scarce data-gathering and analytical resources. Ultimately it should be the administrators who decide the priorities for planning efforts. The implications of the preceding chapters regarding choice of study topics are fairly clear. Studies in the usual mold of manpower and rate-of-return analysis should be considered carefully before being undertaken. This is not to say that they should never be undertaken. High-level macro-studies provide some useful insights (the Hoerr analysis of rates of return played an important role in the case study). But before undertaking applications of the well-known educational planning approaches, it would be well to ask a series of questions. What will the policy outputs of the study be? Can the methodology be modified to provide information on specific policy alternatives? Can the aggregated information produced be related to other, less-aggregative analyses? Will the study tell us anything about how to make specific programs function better or be more efficient? Is this the research that is most needed in this country at this time.

The Nature of Technical Assistance Teams. If technical assistance is to be effective, it should be based upon a workable conceptual framework for educational planning. Hopefully the arguments in favor of a micro-analytical, systems analysis-oriented approach to planning have been persuasive. Members of technical assistance teams should have a thorough understanding of the strengths and weaknesses of both the standard planning approaches and a systems approach such as that advocated here. Going beyond this point, technical assistance teams should be interdisciplinary so as to provide guidance on various aspects of the planning and research process. Teams should generally include economists familiar with public expenditure analysis, persons with statistical ability, and persons with strong abilities in research design and program evaluation. At least one person should be responsible for maintaining liaison with top administrators and helping generate a demand for planning outputs that parallels the supply capability of the planning office. Other advisors with special expertise may be needed for specific problems (for example, education budget specialists and/or costs analysts). While this may sound like a large team, good technical advisors will often possess several of the skills listed above, plus others such as information systems design, educational performance measurement, and so on. The day has past when foreign technical advisors acted as "experts" with right answers to educational planning problems. Relationships between advisors and host-country technicians have tended to become more collegial.[4] In the writer's opinion, the purpose of technical assistance should be to leave behind a cadre of professionals who possess a way of looking at the country's specific educational problems developed through joint participation in planning tasks. Specific answers to policy questions become quickly out of date; it is the process of using data and analysis to cast light on the answers that is important.

Training Educational Planners. An important aspect of technical assistance is the training given by advisors "on the job" through examples to their counterparts. More formal training may be necessary to generate skills and abilities that are needed but not on hand. Formal training can take place either in the country or outside. Obviously this study implies that training should be oriented away from the major conceptual frameworks and toward the kind of planning discussed here. There are few schools if any that embrace such a view of educational planning. Most pure discipline degree-oriented courses provide much irrelevant material and do not offer the sorts of preparation that trainees can put into practice when they return to their jobs. They also tend to teach the well-known, high-level approaches to educational planning. The most important objective of education and training for educational planning is creation of a set of mind or a "way of looking at problems." Degree programs or training courses should give their graduates an outlook that leads to:

    questioning program objectives;
    breaking objectives down to an operational level;
    seeking more effective alternatives to existing practices;

willingness to experiment;

quantifying the inputs, costs, and outputs of programs;

comparing alternatives in terms of their costs and effectiveness;

using simple models;

generating new, policy-relevant data where needed;

using sampling techniques and applying cost-effectiveness principles to selection of study topics and methodology;

reexamining objectives;

restructuring problems;

examining program efficiency and building a program strategy
"from the bottom up" by assuring that programs are operating
effectively.

There is some risk that graduates of planning courses may return
to their planning offices with overly-optimistic expectations of what
a systems approach to planning can accomplish. But if a graduate
has a clear perception of the strengths and weaknesses of planning
tools and approaches and has gained the outlook characterized above,
he will be prepared to use his technical skills judiciously to provide
useful information to decision makers.

Training Administrators. If the purpose of planning is to provide
information for decision makers, and if the information is often
quantitative and presented in the form of technical analyses, then
it is important that administrators be able to interpret and use such
information. At the least, this implies that administrators should be
familiar with a vocabulary of basic concepts of planning such as cost-
effectiveness comparison (instead of cost-minimizing or quality-
maximizing outlooks). They should possess an understanding of the
nature of and need for quantitative, policy-relevant data and should
be able to specify their informational needs clearly to planners,
researchers, and information systems specialists who will provide
the information. They should be sufficiently familiar with sampling
methodologies to understand that a sample-based study can be reasonably reliable and may even possess distinct advantages over full
censuses. If administrators have some familiarity with these and
a few other concepts, then their ability to use the outputs of planning
and communicate with their technical staffs will be greatly enhanced.
It is usually not feasible to send administrators outside the country
for extensive courses, but development of the needed vocabulary of
concepts need not involve a great deal of time or study. If ways can
be found to impart the information quickly and effectively (through
technical assistance, short courses, or preparation of instructional
materials that can be brought to the administrators), it would improve
the environment within which planning takes place and the utilization
of the outputs of planning offices.

140

NOTES

1. "Building a System for Assistance Activities," in E. N. Shiver, ed. Higher Education and Public International Service (Washington, D.C.: American Council on Education, 1967), p. 45.

2. An Introduction to the Economics of Education (London: Allen Lane The Penguin Press, 1970), p. 222.

3. See A. M. Rivlin, Systematic Thinking for Social Action (Washington, D.C.: Brookings Institution, 1971), pp. 86-119, for a discussion of the difficulties of conducting experiments and an argument that, despite the difficulties, experimentation and research are essential for increasing the effectiveness of social services.

4. For an excellent discussion of changes in the nature of technical assistance and the need for interdisciplinary teams, see M. J. Esman and J. D. Montgomery, "Systems Approaches to Technical Cooperation: The Role of Development Administration," Public Administration Review, 24, no. 5 (September/October, 1969): 507-39.

APPENDIX A:
THE MALAYSIAN EDUCATION SYSTEM

Malaysia's education system[1] is, by most standards, one of the best in Southeast Asia and the developing world. Enrollment and retention through the primary and lower secondary cycles are high. In comparison with other developing countries, teacher quality is high, the system is well organized, and supply of facilities and texts is adequate in most cases. This relative good fortune does not, however, mean that there are no problems or needs for planning and change. On the whole the system still follows the British educational pattern, even though some changes have been introduced since independence in 1957. The following sections of this appendix are primarily intended to provide background information that will permit readers to place the case study in Chapters 4 and 5 in context in the system as a whole.

LEGAL FOUNDATION

The Federal Constitution states: "Education is the responsibility of the Federal Government and Parliament is the legislative authority. . . . The right to education is one of the fundamental liberties, as is the right of religious groups to maintain their sectarian schools. . . . All pupils receive equal treatment." The constitution further specifies that, "discrimination on the grounds of race, religion, descent or place of birth is prohibited in schools maintained by the Government or a public body."

The education act of 1961, which is still the principal authorizing act, states the goals of the system as follows:

> The education policy of the Federation originally established in the Educational Ordinance, 1957, is to establish a national system of education which will satisfy the needs of the nation and promote its cultural, social, economic and political development . . . and for the progressive development of an educational system in which the national language is the main medium of instruction.[2]

A HISTORY OF DIVERSITY

One of the principal characteristics of the Malaysian education system is its multiethnic and multilingual makeup. Since independence and before, Malaysia has had four separate educational streams at the primary level, one for each of the major ethnic communities—Malays, Chinese, and Indians—and an English language stream. Secondary education was provided only in English in the public schools and Chinese in private schools supported by the Chinese community, until independence. A Malay language secondary stream was established at independence and Chinese secondary education has dwindled to an inconsequential level.

A policy change made in 1969 calls for the progressive elimination of the English language stream, beginning with the first grade in 1969 and proceeding by one grade each year through the secondary level. This means that the only secondary education available will be in Malay. Elimination of the English language stream, which was ordered following serious racial disturbances in 1969, has caused some upheaval in the education system as well as strong feelings on the part of the non-Malay minorities. To the Chinese and Indians, who tended to excel in the English stream, the policy appears to favor the Malays. To proponents of the change, it is a step toward national linguistic unity.

The earliest form of education in Malaysia was undoubtedly semiformal religious education conducted by the religious hierarchy for the sons of the rulers and the aristocracy. Religious education, which taught mainly the Koran, was later secularized and became the basis for formal education in the Malay language.

English language education began with missionary schools in the early nineteenth century and was continued, with the support of the British Colonial Office, as a means of training the lower- and middle-level bureaucrats and functionaries who would serve as subordinate staffs of government and commercial offices and agencies. In addition private, nonsectarian English language schools, such as the Penang Free School, were established in the nineteenth century.

A few missionary schools also offered classes in the Malay language. The principal roots of Malay education, however, were the Koran schools established throughout the country with the support of the church and the Sultanates. In time their support was assumed by the government. Education for women was not accepted until the twentieth century. In 1938 there were 662 boys' schools and 164 girls' schools in the Malay medium. Since no Malay secondary education was available until recently, Malay children had to learn English in order to pursue their education. A special "remove year" was provided for the language transition.

Early Chinese education was provided by voluntary contributions and fees paid by the Chinese communities. Grants to Chinese schools were first made in 1924 and were extended until most Chinese education was either partially or fully assisted in the 1960s. Public assistance to Chinese secondary education was abolished in 1962, which led to a major decline in the number of Chinese secondary schools and, indirectly, to a decline in enrollment in the Chinese primary stream. A few private Chinese secondary schools linger but are not an important element in the total education picture.

The Indian population, largely of Tamil extraction, originally came to Malaysia as railroad laborers and rubber tappers. Indian vernacular education developed informally on the rubber plantations and was generally very poor in quality. In 1912 a law requiring rubber estates to provide adequate primary education led to some standardization of estate schools, but quality continued to be very low. In 1956 responsibility for the Tamil schools was assumed by the government.

In 1956, prior to independence, a major study of the Malaysian education system was undertaken under the direction of Tun Abdul Razak, then Minister of Education and later to become Prime Minister.[3] The Razak Committee Report established the general guidelines that, for the most part, continue to shape the education system. The Razak Report called for a major effort to increase enrollment, guaranteed education in the vernacular languages for the three ethnic communities, provided for standardized curriculums in all streams and substantially increased financial support for all schools. Free primary education was offered through the first six years of schooling. The government committed itself to provide places for all who chose to seek an education but did not undertake either universal or compulsory primary education. Malay and English were to be compulsory subjects in all streams, teacher training was to be standardized, and conformity with national standards (for example, class size, pupil/teacher ratios, curriculums, syllabuses, hours, and so on) was required. In 1960 a committee chaired by the next Minister of Education, Abdul Rahman Talib, reviewed the Razak Report and made further recommendations in the light of three years' experience.[4] These two documents have set forth the major policy statements on education in Malaysia. Their principal thrust has been toward quantitative and qualitative development and, importantly, toward some unity and uniformity in the fragmented system.

STRUCTURE

The structure of the education system follows a pattern derived from the British: six years of primary schooling followed by three years of lower secondary education (Forms I through III), two years of upper secondary (Forms IV and V), and two years of "post secondary" or university-preparatory schooling called Lower and Upper Form VI. The thirteen years and four levels of education are shown in Figure A.1 as they will appear after full implementation of the policy to eliminate the English language stream.

A major policy change was made in 1966, extending open and free education through nine grades (that is, through the full lower secondary cycle or Form III). The "eleven plus" examination that had previously limited entry to the lower secondary level was abolished and a system of automatic promotion was instituted through the full nine years. This opening of the lower secondary level created an upward surge in enrollment and candidates for upper secondary places, which led to the situation addressed in the case study. The enlarged lower secondary system is called "comprehensive education." During these three years all students are required to take one of four "elective" subjects designed to expose them to practical arts: agriculture, industrial arts, home science and commerce. In practice, few schools offer more than one elective choice for boys and either home science or commerce for girls.

Beyond Form III, the system branches into various specialized streams. The great majority of students remain in the arts and sciences streams of general education, hoping to gain admission to the university or at least to higher level specialized schools. Enrollment in the arts stream greatly exceeds enrollment in the science stream, particularly in the Malay medium, and this is a source of concern for policy makers. A secondary technical stream is offered, which differs only slightly from the science stream except for a limited number of hours of practical technical courses. Secondary vocational education is also offered, but this stream is small. Its enrollment amounts to some 4 percent of the general education stream.

Further diversification takes place after the lower secondary level. Technical colleges (distinct from secondary technical schools) provide quasi-terminal technical education for three years and a poly-technic institute offers a two-year course. Teacher training colleges admit some entrants after Form V, who become primary school teachers after a two-year course. Teacher training colleges also admit students who complete Form VI, for a two-year course preparing lower and upper secondary school teachers. Training for higher level secondary teachers is provided by the Faculties of Education at two universities. This last category of teachers, called "graduates," is supposed to supply half the upper secondary teaching force and all Form VI teachers. Thus far this norm has not been achieved and the distribution of graduate teachers among secondary schools is uneven. A separate secondary technical school, called the MARA Institute of Technology, operates outside the Ministry of Education. This school and other MARA training courses provide occupationally-oriented education for Malays in a wide array of courses.

FIGURE A.1

Structure of the Malaysian Education System[a]

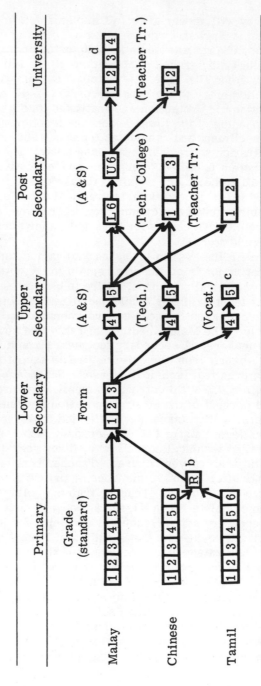

[a]Reflects the pattern that will exist after elimination of the English language medium.
[b]Remove Year for language transition to secondary education in Malay.
[c]Vocational education is a terminal course.
[d]Arts and Science graduates finish University education in three years.

Source: Adapted from Education in Malaysia (1970), p. 18.

146

University education has grown very rapidly since independence. The University of Malaya, which established its principal seat in Kuala Lumpur after Singapore's withdrawal from Malaysia, has grown to full capacity at about 9,000 enrollment. The University of Penang, founded in 1968, has achieved the status of a full higher education institution. The former Agricultural College at Serdang is being upgraded to prepare not only middle-level agricultural technicians but also to provide full university education in agriculture and related specialties. A new National University (Universiti Kebangsaan) has begun operation as a fourth institution of higher education, where Malay will be the only language of instruction and orientation will be toward Malay studies. A fifth institution, the Universiti Islam, is the developmental stage. Some concern has been voiced that expansion of university education has been too rapid and that quality will suffer (or has already begun to suffer). The three main higher education institutions—University of Malaya, University of Penang, and the Agricultural University—have offered primarily English language instruction. As part of the national policy regarding language of instruction, Malay will become the main language in all three. This is another source of concern for some.

ENROLLMENT AND SURVIVAL

Establishment of automatic promotion through nine years has greatly reduced wastage and virtually eliminated repetition. Some 95 percent of each cohort entering primary school completes grade six.* Approximately 50 percent of the original cohort remains in school to the end of Form III. Continued wastage despite automatic promotion (heaviest after grade six), appears to be due to socioeconomic factors. Wastage is greatest among women, in the Malay medium and in the rural areas. A major longitudinal study to determine the causes of wastage has been initiated by the Education Planning and Research Division under the supervision of Alan B. Wilson.[5]

After Form III, access to the upper secondary level is limited by the Lower Certificate of Education examination (LCE). Between 50 and 60 percent of candidates for the LCE and Form IV have been successful in recent years, as discussed at length in Chapter 4. The surge in enrollment, brought about by open access and automatic promotion through Form III, has led to rapid increases in upper

---

*Although single-year population estimates prior to the 1971 Census limited precision, it is estimated that some 95 percent of the relevant population (ages six to seven) enter grade one.

secondary enrollment. Of the 50 percent of each entering cohort that survive through Form III, roughly half (or 25 percent of the entering cohort) gain access to the upper secondary level. Virtually all of these remain in school through Form V. A limited number of unsuccessful candidates for the LCE exam are permitted to repeat Form III and retake the exam, thus there is repetition (as high as 10 percent of Form III enrollment) at this level.

After the upper secondary level is completed, another examination stringently limits entry to the university-preparatory Form VI. This examination, the Malaysian Certificate of Education (MCE), is passed by some 15 percent of candidates. Thus only some 4 percent of each cohort that entered primary school attains Form VI. Most who gain access complete the two-year cycle. As in the case of candidates for the LCE exam, some unsuccessful candidates repeat Form V and attempt the examination a second time. There are also a number of private schools that specialize in "cramming" students for the MCE.

Automatic promotion has been criticized on the grounds that many students merely "pass through" the system for nine years and emerge without a true lower secondary education. Policy statements reflect a concern for consolidating the quantitative gains made in recent years and improving the quality of education. Evaluation of the progress of individual students has tended to be weak. Only one national examination—the Standard Five (that is, grade five) Assessment examination—provides objective evaluation. Despite some concern regarding quality, the Malaysian education system has achieved higher levels of quantitative development (that is, higher enrollment ratios) than other Southeast Asian nations with the exception of Singapore, Hong Kong, and Japan.

EXAMINATIONS

The flow of pupils through the system is regulated by the several major examinations. During the colonial years, examinations were conducted by the Cambridge Examination Syndicate, which administered its Overseas School Certificate and other examinations. Upon independence Malaysia established its own Examinations Syndicate with technical advice and cooperation from Cambridge. More recently the Ford Foundation has sponsored an advisory and training project, conducted by the Educational Testing Service (ETS) of Princeton, N.J. Through this project, Malaysian examinations specialists have been trained in the preparation and use of objective testing methods, the LCE and MCE examinations have been converted from individually-graded test papers to fully-objective, automatically processed standardized examinations. A computer center for processing examinations has also been established. The Malaysian Examination Syndicate is now completely independent of Cambridge. Technical improvements in examinations methodology continue to be made.

At the lowest level of examinations, the Standard Five Assessment examination serves a diagnostic function and does not affect pupil placement. Improvements in the uses of this examination as an instrument for assessing educational quality and effectiveness are under consideration. The principal examinations that affect promotion to higher levels are: (1) The Lower Certificate of Education (LCE), administered at the Form III level and governing access to upper secondary education; (2) The Malaysian Certificate of Education (MCE), administered after Form V and governing entrance to Form VI; (3) The Higher School Certificate (HSC); taken upon completion of Upper Form VI. The last examination affects entrance to the university level. Also offered are the Malaysian Certificate of Vocational Education (MCVE) and other specialized examinations. In some areas such as subject-specific vocational examinations, external examinations from the United Kingdom are still used (for example, the London City and Guilds Examination).

The Malaysian examinations are considered to be of high quality, particularly since the introduction of objective testing with ETS technical assistance. While there are criticisms of excessive domination of the system by examinations, a move away from the use of examinations as at present would involve not only fundamental changes within the education system but also important changes in labor market institutions and attitudes toward possession of academic credentials. The existence of the examinations, whatever one might feel regarding their pedagogical effects, provides an important source of objective data on educational quality and performance. Chapter 4 and Appendix B discuss some research and analytical uses of the exam data.

VOCATIONAL EDUCATION

Limited vocational education was provided in Malaysia beginning in the early twentieth century, for the specific purpose of training technicians for the Railway and Public Works Departments. Four trade schools were later opened in the period from 1926 to 1932, offering three-year training courses at the lower secondary level for mechanics and fitters. Enrollments were small and most graduates found employment in government departments. Following the war and liberation from Japanese occupation, these trade schools were given broader curriculums (machine shop practice, electrical installation, motor engineering, carpentry, bricklaying and cabinet making). Plans and studies at the time of independence in 1956

called for upgrading these early trade schools to become technical
institutes, and for the creation of fourteen new two-year schools
(still at the lower secondary level) to provide a vocational alternative
for those who could not gain entrance to academic lower secondary
education. The new type of schools were called Sekolah Lanjutang
Kampong (rural trade schools). Only six were eventually established.
Other changes were made to elevate the four original technical institutes to the upper secondary level and to extend the Sekolah Lanjutang
Kampong to three years.

Finally, with the elimination of the "eleven plus" or secondary
school entrance examination and establishment of free access to lower
secondary comprehensive education in 1965, a major change was
made. The Sekolah Lanjutang Kampong (which had not been successful)
were eliminated and seven secondary vocational schools were created
at the upper secondary level, offering a two-year course. Admission
was open to all, but in practice the schools tended to serve as a last
resort for those failing to gain access to academic upper secondary
schools. Thus vocational education at the upper secondary level came
into being bearing a legacy from earlier trades training that had been
offered at lower levels and for marginal pupils excluded from the
main stream.

Certification of vocational education was originally provided
by the London City and Guilds Examination and other overseas testing
institutions. The Malaysian Examinations Syndicate established a
national examination—the Malaysian Certificate of Vocational Education (MCVE)—that was nominally the equivalent of the MCE offered
after Form V. The MCVE was set in 1969 for the first cohort of
pupils to complete the course offered in the new schools. Research
on the experience of the early graduating classes necessarily had to
be based on special follow-up studies, since broad sample surveys
could not be expected to find sufficient graduates in the labor force
through random sampling.

Enrollment in the vocational schools was small. Until the late
1960s, only a few hundred graduates were produced each year from
the earlier types of vocational schools. The First Malaysia Plan
(1965-70) called for major expansion of the vocational stream. Enrollment grew from a total of 553 vocational students in 1965 to 2,672
(now in the new type schools) in 1970. This still constituted only
between 3 and 4 percent of total upper secondary enrollment. Many
observers, including the World Bank, felt that many more vocational
schools should be created. The bank's manpower-based studies indicated a "need" for 13,000 vocational graduates each year, which would
require a tenfold increase in vocational enrollment. Other sources
of information, as discussed in Chapter 5, indicated that vocational
education was not producing graduates that were readily employed

150

TABLE A.1

Comparison of Education Expenditures and Total
Federal Expenditures
(in millions of current Malaysian dollars)

Year	Total Federal Recurrent Expenditures	Federal Development Expenditures	Total Education Recurrent Expenditures	Education Development Expenditures
1966	1,619	651	360	63
1967	1,800	625	403	52
1968	1,796	619	404	53
1969	1,933	615	439	43
1970	2,163	725	477	44
1971	2,398	1,085	536	86

Source: Treasury Economic Report, 1972-73, pp. 134, 140, 144.

in the private sector. For this reason, specific policy research on vocational education was needed.

EDUCATIONAL FINANCE

Since education is a federal responsibility, local authorities are not called upon to provide for the costs of education. Some school fees are charged above the Form III level to non-Malay children, but these do not constitute a major source of revenue. The main source of support is the federal budget allocation for the Ministry of Education. Table A.1 shows the total education budget (and the recurrent cost component of that budget) in comparison with the total federal budget for recent years.

Some attempts at program budgeting have been made in Malaysia's Ministry of Education, although that agency has resisted more than others the national policy directives calling for adoption of program budgeting. Some successful attempts at unit cost measurement have been made and included in the national budget estimates and analyses. These unit costs form part of the basis for the cost estimates used in Chapters 4 and 5. On the whole, program budgeting has not been adopted and the presentation and categorization of education budgets still adheres to the line-item approach.

NOTES

1. This section draws upon the following sources. Ministry of Education, Education Planning and Research Division (EPRD), Education in Malaysia (Kuala Lumpur: Dewan Bahasa dan Pustaka, 1967), pp. 5-86. UNESCO/IAU (H. Hayden, ed.) Higher Education and Development in Southeast Asia (Paris: UNESCO, 1967, Vol. II, Country Profiles), pp. 275-396. H. S. Beebout, "The Production Surface for Academic Achievement: An Economic Study of Malaysian Secondary Schools" (Ph.D. dissertation, University of Wisconsin at Madison, 1972), pp. 103-35. I. Lourdesamy, "The Vocational School Program in Malaysia" (Ph.D. dissertation, University of Pittsburgh, 1972). It is also based upon the writer's experience as Ford Foundation advisor to the EPRD from 1969 to 1971. The appendix, and the case study in Chapter 4, consider the education system in West Malaysia alone and exclude the special features of education in the Borneo states.

2. Quoted in Education in Malaysia, op. cit., p. 5.

3. Federal Legislative Council Paper No. 21, 1956.

4. Report of the Education Review Committee, 1960 (Kuala Lumpur: Government Printer, 1964).

5. Jawatankuasa Di Atas Kajian Pendapat Mengenai Pelajaran Dan Masyarakat (Study of opinion about education and society) (Kuala Lumpur: Ministry of Education, 1973).

Late in 1970 the Education Planning and Research Division of
Malaysia's Ministry of Education sponsored a large sample survey
of upper secondary schools. The survey was directed by Harold S.
Beebout, a Fulbright Fellow doing research in Malaysia.[1] The academic research purpose of the study was to investigate production
function relationships between educational inputs, background, or
environmental factors affecting the schools, and a dependent performance variable based upon changes in examination scores in the course
of the two-year upper secondary cycle. EPRD and the Ministry of
Education sponsored the study to gain insights into a number of factors,
notably educational costs, finance, and the supply and distribution of
educational facilities and other inputs. This appendix describes the
study as an example of feasible, mission-oriented research producing
data that are useful for policy analysis as discussed in Chapter 3. It
also provides background information on the source of some of the
data appearing in Chapter 4.

The Secondary School Survey was unusual by any standards
because it gathered data on school inputs, costs, and a quasi-longitudi-
nal measure of performance in a way that permitted cross tabulation
and multivariate analysis. It was also unusual because it produced
disaggregated data on educational costs by major component. Finally
it was unusual for Malaysia because it was based on approximately
a 25 percent sample rather than a full census of upper secondary
schools. In terms of the characteristics of useful data discussed in
Chapter 3, the survey data are longitudinal, disaggregated, and related
to both costs and performance. As a basis for systems analysis,
however, the data set produced has a major limitation: the data do
not describe clear policy alternatives between which decision makers
are asked to choose. Comparisons must be made between groups of
schools that possess more or less of some inputs and exhibit different
performance within the uniform framework of the upper secondary
school regulations. The study found that there is sufficient variance
in a number of variables to permit meaningful analysis. In addition,
the data are useful for descriptive purposes and offered a number of
insights not available from regularly reported data.

The universe from which the sample was drawn was all public
secondary schools that had a full upper secondary level (Forms IV
and V) in 1969. This statistical population of 377 schools was stratified
by medium of instruction (Malay and English) and by state. A propor-
tional random sample of 189 schools was then drawn from this sample

frame, thus the techniques of statistical inference from sample statistics to population parameters could be applied. The sample size was considered sufficient for statistical reliability. The unit of observation for the EPRD survey was the individual school, although Beebout carried on his production function analysis on the basis of examination performance of individual pupils in the sample schools.

The data on the 89 sample schools were compiled from three different sources. One source was a pair of questionnaires prepared at EPRD. The first questionnaire was distributed to headmasters of the sample schools and completed by them from their records. A complementary questionnaire was administered by a team of enumerators (members of the State Education Office staffs) trained to cross check the headmasters' responses and make their own observations about qualitative factors and variables possibly affected by headmasters' biases. Together the questionnaires provided data on the educational inputs offered by each school in the previous year, including teacher qualifications and experience, enrollment details, quantitative and qualitative data on school facilities, and background variables such as whether the school was urban or rural, single or double session, and so on. Since the survey was sponsored by the ministry and each school was visited by a team of enumerators, responses were received from all 89 schools. Follow-up spot checks and observations of the field enumeration process indicated that the data were accurate and complete.

The second source of data was the audited accounts of the individual schools, made available by the Finance and Accounts Division of the Ministry of Education. Annual audits are required of all schools in Malaysia. These are conducted by private accounting firms approved by the ministry. While the audits provide a useful source of cost data, lack of consistency in audit procedure creates some problems in the way costs are categorized. Considerable effort was devoted in the survey and analysis of data to making the cost data internally consistent and compatible. For the purposes of the survey and subsequent analysis, the cost data were considered reliable.[2]

The third source of data was the scores of the pupils in the sample schools on the LCE and MCE examinations, which were made available by the Examinations Syndicate. It was possible to "track" most students in each sample school from their LCE exam, taken upon entering the upper secondary level, to the MCE exam taken upon completing the level. This affords a longitudinal measure of educational performance, even though data were collected on a cross-sectional basis. Each of the achievement test batteries (LCE and MCE) is prepared by the Examinations Syndicate. Comparable examinations are given in English and Malay languages. The examinations are considered to be both technically sound and carefully administered and scored. While there may be reasons to question exactly what achievement tests measure, these tests can be considered reliable instruments to measure whatever is meant by "achievement" in the Malaysian education system.

The methodology for obtaining an index of performance on the basis of comparisons of averages is somewhat complex.[3] Beebout cites a study by Dyer, Linn, and Patton of the Educational Testing Service as the methodological source.[4] The method involved establishing a regression line for the paired entering and leaving scores of all students in a particular school. This regression line was then compared with the "grand" regression line for the medium as a whole. The difference between the two lines, measured at the mean on the LCE examination, gives the performance index. In other words the better the regression line of leaving upon entering scores for a particular school compares with the overall regression line, the more the school has done to effect achievement gains in its pupils during the upper secondary cycle. Beebout's preliminary report provides a fuller explanation, diagram, and numerical example.[5]

These three sources of data covered a wide array of variables. All variables were specific to the unit of observation (the school, for EPRD's purposes) so cross tabulations of variables could be performed. In Beebout's multivariate analysis of the data, a limited set of variables proved to have explanatory power in terms of the dependent variable (the performance index). Other variables gathered in the survey were of considerable information value for EPRD. Table B.1 presents the variable list used by Beebout in his model. Other variables gathered but not used in the production function study can be grouped in the following categories:

Variables relating to physical facilities and space utilization;
Variables relating to quality of science facilities;
Variables relating to adequacy and accessibility of the library;
Variables relating to student motivation;
Variables relating to headmaster's administrative style;
Detailed variables on teachers' utilization: subjects taught, hours spent in each subject, and so on;
Detailed cost variables (omitted from Beebuot's model); expenditures from per capita grants for recurring nonsalary expenses, by category; expenditures from per capita grants for nonrecurring expenses, by category; total cash assets on hand;
Detailed variables on examination performance by major subject area.

Beebout was successful in demonstrating that there are production function relationships between educational inputs and academic

TABLE B.1

Variables From the Secondary School Survey Used in a Linear Model of Student Achievement

Dependent Variable

    Educational performance index

Student Background Variable

    Student entering scores on LCE exam

Outside-the-School Educational Inputs

    Percent of non-Malay students
    Percent of students from agrarian family backgrounds
    Location near an urban center
    Boarding school or not

School Inputs

    Percent qualified teachers
    Average years of teacher experience
    Class size
    Teacher motivation
    Percent of library use
    Quality of library materials
    Building age

Conditioning Factors

    Girls' school, boys' school, or coed
    Double or single session school
    Size of school
    Percent of students in science stream

Source: Beebout, "The Production Surface for Academic Achievement," p. 250.

achievement, but he emphasizes that education has broader objectives than simply the production achievement gains.[6] The most important explanatory variables were teacher training and experience, although other variables showed significant relationships with the dependent variable. Beyond this limited research objective, he also found that the data indicated several points regarding resource allocation and educational policy.[7] These concerned: (1) the efficiency of the school input mix; (2) equity in the provision of school inputs; and (3) economies of scale.

Beebout pursued the analysis of input and output relationships to determine the "marginal achievement product" per unit of input for different input variables. When these marginal products were divided by the costs of the inputs, cost-effectiveness ratios or achievement elasticities of investment in different inputs were obtained. Table B.2 shows the cost-effectiveness ratios for a limited set of significantly related independent variables.

The full data set can be used for many other purposes in addition to those explored by Beebout. One of the principal reasons why the EPRD sponsored the study was to gain information on the adequacy of the existing system of per capita grants to schools for recurrent nonteaching expenses and nonrecurring expenses (for example, purchases of office equipment, teaching equipment, and so on). This and other uses of the cost data were largely excluded from Beebout's production function study. The data on per pupil costs of the upper secondary level were much more informative than data previously available and are used in the model presented in Appendix C.

Other uses of the descriptive data could be made. For example, the data on quality of physical facilities, laboratories, libraries, and so on could be used as a basis for estimating investment needs. No other data on these subjects were available. Explorations of the internal efficiency of upper secondary education could be pursued farther than Beebout did, on the basis of some of the detailed cost

TABLE B.2

Gains in Achievement Percentage Points
Per Unit of Expenditure

Input Variable	Malay Medium	English Medium
Percent qualified teachers	.010	—
Untrained teachers	.083	.144
Years' teaching experience	-.142	.011
Class size	.028	—
Boarding school	—	.0006
Double sessions	.077	—

Source: Beebout, "The Production Surface for Academic Achievement," p. 197.

157

data. Policy questions relating to the proportion of enrollment in science as opposed to arts stream education could be investigated. And a great deal of data was generated on academic performance in individual subjects on the examinations, which would permit analysis of production function relationships at a more detailed level than Beebout's investigation of the "aggregate" production function for academic achievement.

In terms of the characteristics of policy-relevant data discussed in Chapter 3, this study demonstrates that it is feasible to gather data of the sort recommended. The cost of the study was not particularly great. Approximately one man year of senior analysts' time was required for survey design, execution of preliminary analysis of the data (nine months of Beebout's time plus the equivalent of perhaps three man months devoted to various aspects of the study by the writer). Subsequent analysis of the data by Beebout required approximately one additional man year plus computer time for the analysis. The EPRD staff was involved in preparation of the questionnaires and the three-day training session for field enumerators. Total time spent by education officers from the individual states in training and field enumeration was less than three man months. If one considers, however, that the time devoted by Ministry of Education officials did not detract from the regular performance of their duties, then the opportunity cost of this time is virtually zero and the total cost of the study is low.

NOTES

1. The data gathered were used in Beebout's Ph.D. dissertation, "The Production Surface for Academic Achievement: An Economic Study of Malaysian Secondary Schools," (Madison, Wisc.: University of Wisconsin, Department of Economics, 1972). A technical description with the questionnaire used and preliminary tabulations of the data are provided in Beebout, "EPRD Secondary School Survey—Preliminary Report," Kuala Lumpur: EPRD, May, 1971. Mimeographed. The writer, then Ford Foundation advisor to the EPRD, took part in aspects of planning and supervision of the study.

2. Beebout, "EPRD Secondary School Survey—Preliminary Report," op. cit., pp. 81-91, provides a detailed description of the nature and treatment of the audited account data.

3. Ibid., pp. 93-94.

4. H. S. Dyer, R. L. Linn, and M. J. Patton, Feasibility Study of Educational Performance Indicators (Princeton: Educational Testing Service, 1967), cited in Beebout, ibid., p. 93.

5. Ibid., p. 94.

6. Beebout, "The Production Surface for Academic Achievement," op. cit., pp. 217-18.

7. Ibid., pp. 215-16. Beebout emphasizes that the suggestive findings of the study should be investigated further before policy decisions are based upon them.

APPENDIX C:
A SIMPLIFIED PUPIL-FLOW MODEL
FOR THE PUBLIC EDUCATION SYSTEM
OF WEST MALAYSIA

This appendix presents a brief description of a very simple pupil-flow model of the Malaysian public education system and tables derived from the model under alternative assumptions regarding the rate of access to the upper secondary level. The tables provide the basis for some of the calculations presented in Chapter 4. A more complete description of the model, its data requirements and further uses is found in the writer's doctoral dissertation.[1]

The model belongs to the family of simulation models. It was programmed by the Malaysian Examination Syndicate, in IBM Report Program Generator language (RPG), for use on the Syndicate's IBM 360-20. Recalling the discussion of approaches to educational planning in Chapter 1, this model is essentially a mechanized form of a "quantitative projections" approach. It permits projections of enrollment, wastage, teacher requirements and recurrent costs under alternative assumptions about population growth, proportion of eligible children who enter grade one, rate of promotion and wastage, pupil teacher ratios, and unit costs.

There are three separate modules or submodels: (1) enrollment and wastage, (2) teacher requirements, and (3) recurrent costs. The model could easily be extended to include university-level enrollment (now omitted), or by adding a module to indicate the capital cost implications of enrollment increases. It should be emphasized that the model is merely descriptive and incorporates no optimizing techniques. The major parameters are determined externally and can be changed individually to show the effects of a single policy change.

A number of simplifications in the real-world situation were made, some for sheer convenience and some for lack of detailed data. (One of the results of the modelling exercise was identification of several key data series, especially cost data, that would enhance understanding of the Malaysian education system.) Various peripheral types of education were excluded from the calculations or combined under broader rubrics. For example, several sixth form technical schools were combined under a single heading. The complexities of transfers of students from one vernacular language stream at the primary level, to a language transition or "remove" year, and ultimately to Form I, were omitted. Flows of repeaters at the Form III and Form V levels (that is, those who could not gain access to lower and upper secondary levels) were dealt with in a crude fashion, which makes it appear that enrollment in Form III actually exceeds enrollment in Form II in the preceding year. Detail on enrollment in the several vernacular language streams at the primary level was omitted, partly due to data problems but also because one language stream (English) was being eliminated. All private education was omitted because private enrollment is relatively small in Malaysia, and because it represents no direct cost to the government. While these simplifications limit the usefulness of the model in some ways, they do not impair the model's principal purposes of projecting enrollment growth, teacher needs, and expenditures in the public education system.

Flows of pupils from year to year are based upon historical data, which show the coefficients of transition (that is, promotion rates from grade to grade) to be quite stable at most levels. Historically based transition ratios provide a basis for projecting the system's growth assuming no change in existing patterns and policies. The implications of various policy changes, such as a change in the proportion of students admitted to Form IV, can be traced by changing the relevant ratio and examining the effects of the change in the several modules of the model.

In addition to the transition ratios discussed above, other data inputs include: (1) demographic data on the population eligible for grade one (the population at least six years but less than seven years of age); (2) data on enrollment at all levels of the system for a particular starting year (in this case 1970); (3) teacher:pupil ratios; (4) estimated withdrawals from the teaching force for death, retirement, or other reasons; and (5) unit costs (excluding capital costs) for each educational level and type in the model.

The model permits five-year projections. If longer-range projections were desired, then the last year's enrollment of one run could be entered as the beginning year vector for another. (Projections of the six-year age group would also be needed.)

The tables below are "output" from the enrollment and cost modules under alternative assumptions regarding access to Form IV. Tables C.1 and C.2 are based upon a 50 percent rate of promotion from Form III to Form IV; Tables C.3 and C.4 assume a 60 percent rate. The tables are included here to illustrate one use of the model and to present the background data for calculations appearing in Chapter 4.

The "level" column in Tables C.1 and C.3 indicates the standard or grade for each row. Transition ratios are historically derived except for the ratio from Form III to Form IV. The beginning year vector shows actual enrollment in 1970. Projected enrollment is shown in the columns headed by years, 1971 through 1975. The wastage columns show the difference between enrollment in a given grade and enrollment in the next higher grade in the following year (read downward and to the right). Wastage figures provide an educational profile of school leavers who enter the labor force.

161

TABLE C.1

Sample Run of Enrollment Model Assuming 50 Percent Access to Form IV

Model:1: Primary and Secondary Enrollment and Wastage Excluding Teacher Training

Level	Transition Ratio	Beginning Year Vector 1970	1971	Wastage	1972	Wastage	1973	Wastage	1974	Wastage	1975	Wastage
Age 6 +	0.940	280262	283730	17024	287421	17245	291831	17510	296444	17787	301473	18088
STD 1	0.990	261152	266706	2612	270176	2667	274321	2702	278657	2743	283385	2787
STD 2	0.980	256449	258540	5129	264039	5171	267474	5281	271578	5349	275870	5432
STD 3	0.980	253084	251320	5062	253369	5026	258758	5067	262125	5175	266146	5243
STD 4	0.970	232115	248022	6963	246294	7441	248302	7389	253583	7449	256883	7607
STD 5	0.950	218004	225152	10900	240581	11258	238905	12029	240853	11945	245976	12043
STD 6		200665	207104		213894		228552		226960		228810	
Total		1421469	1456844		1488353		1516312		1533756		1557070	
Form remove	0.250	46537	50166	70233	51776	72486	53474	74863	57138	79993	56740	79436
Form 1	0.650	128707	130432	6435	134618	6522	139031	6731	148559	6952	147524	7428
Form 2	0.950	107348	122272	5367	123910	6114	127887	6196	132079	6394	141131	6604
Form 3	0.950	95943	101981		116158		117715		121493		125475	
Total		378535	404851		426462		438107		459269		470870	
Form 3		95943	101981	47972	116158	50991	117715	58079	121493	58858	125475	60747
Form 4	0.500	43089	47972		50991		58079		58858		60747	
Form 5	1.010	46614	43520		48452		51501		58660		59447	
Total		89703	91492		99443		109580		117518		120194	
Form L6	0.150	5871	6992	39622	6528	36992	7268	41184	7725	43776	8799	49861
Form U6	1.000	4769	5871		6992		6528		7268		7725	
Total		10640	12863		13520		13796		14993		16524	
F 6 Tech 1	0.025	841	1165	21	1088	29	1211	27	1288	30	1467	32
F 6 Tech 2	0.975	677	820		1136		1061		1181		1256	
Total		1518	1985		2224		2272		2469		2723	
University	0.700	1111	3338	1431	4110	1761	4894	2098	4570	1958	5088	2180

Source: Data from a computer run of the flow model developed by the author.

TABLE C.2

Sample Run of Cost Model Assuming 50 Percent Access to Form IV
(in thousands of dollars)

	MODEL 3: Recurrent Cost Estimates by Level				
	1971	1972	1973	1974	1975
Primary enrolment	1456844	1488353	1516312	1533756	1557070
Primary recurrent cost (@ $155 PPPA+)	$225811	$230695	$235028	$237732	$241346
Lower secondary enrolment (Forms R-III)	404851	426462	438107	459269	470870
Lower secondary recurrent cost (@ $190 PPPA+)	$73922	$81028	$83240	$87261	$89465
Upper secondary enrolment	91492	99443	109580	117518	120194
Upper secondary recurrent cost (@ $195 PPPA+)	$17841	$19391	$21368	$22916	$23438
Form VI enrolment	12863	13520	13796	14993	16524
Form VI Average Recurrent cost (@ $600 PPPA+)	$7718	$8112	$8278	$8996	$9914
Other Form VI technical enrolment	1985	2224	2272	2469	2723
Form VI tech. recurrent cost (@ $3000 PPPA+ IN)	$5955	$6672	$6816	$7407	$8169

Note: PPPA = per pupil per year.

Source: Data from a computer run of the flow model developed by the author.

163

TABLE C.3

Sample Run of Enrollment Model Assuming 60 Percent Access to Form IV

Model 1: Primary and Secondary Enrollment and Wastage Excluding Teacher Training

Level	Transition Ratio	Beginning Year Vector 1970	1971	Wastage	1972	Wastage	1973	Wastage	1974	Wastage	1975	Wastage
Age 6 +	0.940	280262	283730	17024	287421	17245	291831	17510	296444	17787	301473	18088
STD 1	0.990	261152	266706	2612	270176	2667	274321	2702	278657	2743	283385	2787
STD 2	0.980	256449	258540	5129	264039	5171	267474	5281	271578	5349	275870	5432
STD 3	0.980	253084	251320	5062	253369	5026	258758	5067	262125	5175	266146	5243
STD 4	0.980	232115	248022		246294		248302		253583		256883	
STD 5	0.970	218004	225152	6963	240581	7441	238905	7389	240853	7449	245976	7607
STD 6	0.950	200665	207104	10900	213894	11258	226552	12029	226960	11945	228810	12043
Total		1421469	1456844		1488353		1516312		1533756		1557070	
Form remove	0.250	46537	50166	70233	51776	72486	53474	74863	57138	79993	56740	79436
Form 1	0.650	128707	130432	6435	134618	6522	139031	6731	148559	6952	147524	7428
Form 2	0.950	107348	122272	5367	123910	6114	127887	6196	132079	6394	141131	6604
Form 3	0.950	95943	101981		116158		117715		121493		125475	
Total		378535	404851		426462		438107		459269		470870	
Form 3	[0.600]	95943	101981	38377	116158	40792	117715	46463	121493	47086	121475	48597
Form 4	1.010	43089	57566		61189		69695		70629		72896	
Form 5		46614	43520		58142		61801		70392		71335	
Total		89703	101086		119331		131496		141021		144231	
Form L6	0.150	5871	6992	39622	6528	36992	8721	49421	9270	52531	10559	59833
Form U6	1.000	4769	5871		6992		6528		8721		9270	
Total		10640	12863		13520		15249		17991		19829	
F 6 Tech 1	0.025	841	1165	21	1088	29	1454	27	1545	36	1760	39
F 6 Tech 2	0.975	677	820		1136		1061		1418		1506	
Total		1518	1985		2224		2515		2963		3266	
University	0.700	1111	3338	1431	4110	1761	4894	2098	4570	1958	6105	2616

Source: Data from a computer run of the flow model developed by the author.

TABLE C.4

Sample Run of Cost Model Assuming 60 Percent Access to Form IV
(in thousands of dollars)

| | MODEL 3: Recurrent Cost Estimates by Level | | | |
	1971	1972	1973	1974	1975
Primary enrolment	1456844	1488353	1516312	1533756	1557070
Primary recurrent cost (@ $155 PPPA)	$225811	$230695	$235028	$237732	$241346
Lower secondary enrolment (Forms R-III)	404851	426462	438107	459269	470870
Lower secondary recurrent cost (@ $199 PPPA)	$76922	$81028	$83240	$87261	$89465
Upper secondary enrolment	101086	119331	131496	141021	144231
Upper secondary recurrent cost (@ $195 PPPA)	$19712	$23270	$25642	$27499	$28125
Form VI enrolment	12663	13520	15249	17991	19829
Form VI average recurrent cost (@ $600 PPPA)	$7718	$8112	$9149	$10795	$11897
Other Form VI Technical enrolment	1985	2224	2515	2963	3266
Form VI technical recurrent cost (@ $3000 PPPA)	$5955	$6672	$7645	$8889	$9798

Note: PPPA = per pupil per year.

Source: Data from a computer run of the flow model developed by the author.

165

In the cost models (Tables C.2 and C.4), total enrollment for each level, derived from the enrollment model, is shown. This is simply multiplied by the recurrent cost per pupil year for that level to obtain the total cost. The submodels showing teacher requirements are not included here.

NOTE

1. R. McMeekin, Jr., "Analysis of Educational Expenditures in Developing Countries," (Ph.D. dissertation, Harvard University, 1973), pp. 288-333.

The principal policy guidance that the major approaches to
educational planning provide is on how investment should be allocated
between different sorts of education. The rate-of-return approach,
in particular, tells us that investment should be reallocated from
low-return to high-return types of education until the rates of return
to the marginal dollar invested in each type of education are equal.
It has been argued in the text that such information, while useful,
is of limited importance; and that economists and planners should
give attention to other sorts of expenditure analysis, including examination of what Leibenstein has called X-efficiency.[1]

The purpose of this appendix is to indicate, on the basis of
some extremely rough, back-of-an-envelope calculations, the possible
magnitude of allocative efficiency gains from reallocating educational
investment in Malaysia; and to compare these with a few partial indicators of potential X-efficiency gains. The precedent for such a
quantitative comparison of the importance of X-efficiency and allocative efficiency is Leibenstein's original article, plus other literature
on the gains from reallocating resources in the private sector.[2] The
subject of these studies is allocative inefficiency due to monopoliza-
tion of industry.

On the basis of a number of strong assumptions, the authors
attempt to measure the consumer's surplus lost when monopolies
limit output and sell at prices above average costs. Figure D.1,
after Leibenstein and Harberger, shows the welfare loss or the
potential allocative efficiency gain from reallocation.[3] The quantity
q' represents the monopoly output, which is sold at price p'. The
competitive situation would involve greater allocation of resources
to production of the output in question, producing the quantity q.
Costs are assumed to be constant and the equilibrium price, p, is
equal to average costs. The welfare gain or consumers' surplus
that would result from reallocation is measured by the triangle a b c.
The authors found that this gain was small.

For various reasons, some theoretical and some due to data
scarcities, the quantitative comparison attempted here is very crude,
even in comparison with the admittedly approximate studies cited.

1. We are looking here at allocative efficiency within one public
sector and must assume that the overall allocation to the sector is
an efficient one; that is, that the return to educational investment as
a whole is equal to the opportunity cost of capital in other public and
private sectors.

FIGURE D.1

Allocative Efficiency Gain from Reallocation

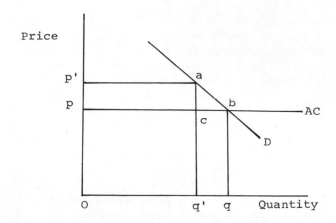

2. Large and sustained overinvestment in one sort of education is a possibility here, but would not be in the private sector. In other words we cannot assume that the forces of competition drive excess capacity out of production as we can in the case of competitive industry. This creates a difficulty of interpretation of the "efficiency gaps" arising from misallocation of educational investment. Figure D.2 shows the situation. Assuming two kinds of education, E1 and E2, with high and low rates of return, respectively, theory tells us that efficiency is maximized by shifting investment from E2 to E1 until greater supplies of E1 graduates and reducation of E2 graduates lead to an equalization of returns. In the left portion of the figure, limited output of E1 leads to a rate of return higher than the opportunity cost of capital, OCC. Increasing output would lead to a welfare gain analogous to the situation in Figure D.1; b c d measures the efficiency gain. The situation regarding E2 is different. Inefficient allocation here has led to overproduction of E2 graduates, so that the marginal return of E2 is below the opportunity cost of capital. Interpretation of the welfare loss is ambiguous. The whole area f g h i represents a loss of "opportunity returns." But in a situation of high unemployment, the area of g h q q' might represent added receipts to otherwise unemployed E2 graduates. Resolution of this theoretical problem would be interesting, but given the other problems that exist, would not greatly aid us in measuring potential allocative efficiency gains.

168

FIGURE D.2

Allocative Efficiency Gains from Reallocation between
Two Types of Education

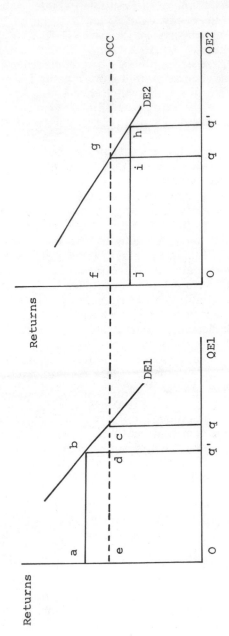

3. The magnitude of the welfare gain depends upon the elasticity of demand for different types of education. In the Malaysian case we are concerned with five major types (E1 . . . E5), the elasticities of which are unknown. Various bits of information might provide a basis for intuitive estimates of demand elasticities. O. D. Hoerr found that rapidly-rising unemployment rates for secondary graduates followed increases in supply, which suggests a low elasticity of demand (or "sticky wage rates," or both).[4] One feels intuitively that the elasticity of demand for primary graduates is somewhat higher, although low overall employment rates in Malaysia suggest that a change in the price of labor would bring about a less-than-equal percentage change in employment (that is, an elasticity of 1.0 would probably be a maximum).

4. The data at hand do not permit measurement of welfare gains in a theoretically clear way. Welfare gain is a function of prices of the outputs (E1 . . . E5 in this case), the actual cost of the outputs, the quantities of the outputs, and the elasticities of demand.[5] As noted, we do not know the elasticities of demand. The prices of the outputs present several difficulties, since we are dealing here with discounted lifetime benefits of education. Hoerr's 1967 data (the only ones available) cannot be readily adapted to this sort of analysis. The outputs of E1 . . . E5 are not homogeneous, thus we are dealing with different submarkets. The data on costs of producing graduates of E1 . . . E5 are very weak. Even the total investment in each cohort of graduates has been estimated very roughly in the analysis below, since the budget data do not permit identification of investment by type of education.

If time and data permitted, it would be interesting to explore the potential gain from reallocating educational investment in greater depth. For purposes of the present rough comparison with partial indications of X-efficiency gains (for which there is no theoretical maximum), the effort is not justified by the information added.

A ROUGH APPROXIMATION OF ALLOCATIVE EFFICIENCY GAINS

A crude way to circumvent the problems above is to consider the returns to a one-year marginal investment under different assumptions. On the one hand we can readily measure the implied annual returns to a year's investment in education assuming continuation of the present balance of expenditure and enrollment between different levels of education. Given two strong assumptions— that the known rates of returns (1967) are still fairly representative of the labor market situation; and that the social returns to investment are received on an equal annual basis—then the total implied return to education under the present allocation of investment is equal to the sum of the products of the investments by level, multiplied by their corresponding returns. On the other hand, if we assume that all rates of return were equalized (at the same rate as the opportunity cost of capital), the return is measured by the product of the total yearly capital and recurrent investment in education and the opportunity cost of capital.

Table D.1 shows such a comparison for that portion of investment in education for which we know the rates of return (that is, excluding general administrative costs and other expenditures that would not be directly affected by reallocation, such as expenditures on examinations, scholarships, maintenance of overseas student centers, and so on). The "Expenditure" or investment column has been estimated by the writer on the basis of the 1971 Expenditure Budget for capital and recurrent costs, with the exclusions mentioned.* The "Rates Assuming Present Allocations" column shows the rates of return observed by Hoerr, based on 1967 data.[6]

The "Returns Assuming Present Allocations" column shows the product of the first two columns. The last column shows total returns under the alternative assumption that returns were equalized at an assumed rate of 10 percent per year.[†]

There is only a small difference between the implied returns to an additional year's investment under the two sets of assumptions. Equalizing the rates of return would produce additional social benefits of $1.8 million per year. If the spread between rates of return to different levels had been wider, then the welfare gains from reallocation would have been larger. This is to say that, in countries where major misallocations between types of education exist, the importance of rate-of-return analysis and reallocation would be greater. For example, a rate-of-return study in Uganda in 1965 found the following spread between rates: primary, 66 percent;

---

*The investment estimates are rough because budget data do not identify expenditures by level clearly.

†Ten percent is the opportunity cost of capital used by Hoerr (op. cit., p. 259), based on studies by the Economic Planning Unit. The true equalization point would be the average of the observed returns weighted by the amount of investment in each type of education and the corresponding demand elasticity. The average, weighted only by the amount of investment in each level (that is, assuming all demand elasticities were equal), is 9.7 percent. Ten percent is thus a reasonable locus for equalization of returns.

TABLE D.1

Comparison of Annual Returns to Educational Investment in Malaysia Assuming
Present Allocations and Reallocations to Equalize Returns

Level of Education	Estimated Expenditure, 1971 (millions of dollars)[a]	Rates of Return Assuming Present Allocations (percent)[b]	Returns Assuming Present Allocations (millions of dollars)[c]	Returns Assuming Reallocation and Equalized Rates of Return (millions of dollars)[d]
Primary	250.3	8.2	20.5	e
Lower secondary	91.3	15.6	14.2	e
Upper secondary	19.8	15.3	3.0	e
Form VI	5.5	12.8	0.7	e
University	59.0	5.8	3.4	e
Total	425.9		40.8	$42.6

aRecurrent and capital expenditures allocable to each level are estimated roughly by the writer because available budget data do not permit accurate measurement by level. The bases for the estimates include: Malaysian Treasury Department, Expenditure Budget, 1971, pp. 415-22; Second Malaysia Plan, 1971-75 (Kuala Lumpur: Government Printing Office, 1973, pp. 222-42), and other partial data.

bNet marginal social returns by level of education, based on 1967 data, as calculated by Hoerr, op. cit., p. 260.

cImplied annual returns, assuming equal returns each year following the investment (col. 1 x col. 2).

dImplied annual returns assuming reallocation of expenditure to equalize returns to all levels at 10 percent (the opportunity cost of capital assumed by Hoerr, op. cit., p. 259.

eReturns to each level not known due to lack of data on demand elasticities.

172

lower secondary, 22 percent; higher secondary, 78 percent; university, 12 percent.[7] One might argue, on the other hand, that if micro-analyses of the sort illustrated in Chapters 4 and 5 had been performed in such countries, the degree of misallocation might never have become so great.

PARTIAL ESTIMATES OF X-EFFICIENCY GAINS

With the potential allocative efficiency gain of $1.8 million in social returns in mind, let us compare this estimate with a few limited indicators of possible X-efficiency gains, that is through internal changes within levels of education rather than shifts of expenditure between levels. The study by Harold S. Beebout, referred to in Chapter 4, provides various data on upper secondary schools that indicate that X-efficiency gains might be achieved at this level in Malaysia.[8] Let us examine some of the possible areas of improvement and their cost implications, recalling that the theoretical maximum X-efficiency gain cannot be determined since both cost savings and improvements in effectiveness can lead to X-efficiency improvements.

1. Class size is unrelated to academic performance in the English medium, but changes in average enrollment per class have a significant impact upon per pupil costs. The norm for class size in both media is 40 pupils in Malaysian lower and upper secondary schools. Average enrollment per class was 36 in Malay medium and 39 in English medium (with standard deviations of 4 and 5 pupils, respectively). Smaller classes were associated with better performance in the Malay medium but in the English medium "the effect on achievement was zero."[9] This was true throughout the range of plus or minus one standard deviation for this variable. The per pupil cost of decreasing average class size by one pupil (or the cost saving from adding a pupil) was $5.43. It is recognized that there may be reasons for reducing class size that are unrelated to academic achievement as measured by test scores.[10] Still the possibility of effecting cost savings by increasing class size (perhaps, for example, by giving lectures once to large groups instead of repeating them for 40-pupil classes) is an area of potential X-efficiency improvement. If increasing average class size by one pupil affected 40,000 pupils in English medium upper secondary, the cost saving would be $214,000. The same cost relationship was observed for lower secondary schools as for upper secondary. (The effect of class size on performance at the lower secondary level is not known, however.) If it is assumed that average class size could be changed by one pupil at the lower secondary level with no ill effect on performance,

then the potential cost saving from this change, assuming 150,000 English medium pupils were affected, would be $814,000. The potential cost saving from this single change alone, affecting only the lower and upper secondary levels, would thus be $1.0 million in comparison with a total efficiency gain from reallocation between levels of $1.8 million.

2. Beebout found that certain combinations of university-trained teachers and more experienced teachers had a significant impact upon the performance variable while other combinations did not. If a school had an average number of university-trained teachers and relatively experienced teachers, then increments of either had little effects on performance. But if the school had shortages of one or the other, the achievement benefits from adding more of the scarce factor (training or experience) were high.[11] It is impossible to estimate how much cost savings might be, since this depends upon many varying factors. It is clear, however, that substantial improvements in performance might be gained at very low (or zero) costs by shifting academically qualified teachers and experienced teachers around to achieve effective combinations.

3. Significant economies of scale were observed, especially for administrative costs. Scale economies were observed in the enrollment range from 250 to 1,500 pupils.[12] Beebout notes that "the estimated cost curves indicate the average non-teacher salary cost of operating a school with total enrollment of 250 is almost $22.00 higher [per pupil] than for a school with a total enrollment of 1,000."[13] In many cases it would not be possible or desirable to consolidate small rural schools, because pupils would then have to travel long distances in order to attend. Where opportunities for consolidation existed, or where arrangements such as administrative teams were possible, the potential impact on costs would be significant. Average size of the surveyed schools was 972 pupils.[14] If, by a conservative estimate, 10 percent of the enrollment in lower and upper secondary schools was affected by consolidation, with a cost impact of one half the extreme figure given above or $11.00 per pupil, then the total cost saving would be on the order of $460.000.

4. Provision of hostels makes it possible for pupils from distant rural areas to attend secondary schools and specialized schools. It is sometimes thought, in addition, that the academic environment of hostel life has a positive effect upon academic achievement. The cost of providing hostel accommodations is very high. Operating costs per hostel place were estimated to be $265 in 1971 and the total cost of hostel facilities amounted to $3.9 million.[15] Beebout found that living in a hostel had no significant impact upon academic achievement.[16] Provision of hostel facilities for pupils who could not otherwise attend secondary schools will continue to be necessary and

174

desirable for reasons not associated with achievement. But the objectives of providing hostel places should be carefully examined. Creation of boarding facilities for achievement-related purposes is not a cost-effective course of action. If the present 15,000 pupils in boarding were reduced, the cost saving to the ministry would approach $0.27 million per 1,000 places eliminated.

5. Beebout analyzed the performance and cost impact of providing disadvantaged schools with inputs equal to the average for all schools.[17] The effect of equalizing school inputs was to improve the poorer schools' achievement, but also to increase costs per pupil by $152. If only those variables were changed that affected performance significantly (and, in particular, if the percentage of pupils in boarding was not changed) then a cost saving of $40 per pupil would be achieved. While the results of such hypothetical exercises based on data from a single survey should be used with great caution, and the cost and performance differences depend heavily upon the norm chosen as desirable, the results indicate clearly that X-efficiency gains of some magnitude could be achieved.

6. Data presented in Chapter 4 (Tables 4.11 and 4.12) showed that the highest cost quartile of schools had performance scores equal to the mean for all schools. The survey data show differences in per pupil costs between the highest cost quartile of schools and the middle two quartiles of $80 per pupil in the Malay medium (with average performance scores virtually the same). If the costs of the high cost quartile could in fact be reduced to the mean costs for all schools with no negative effect on performance, the savings would amount to $1.6 million.

7. Various fragmentary indications of X-inefficiency are found elsewhere. The expected income value of the "best" vocational trade specialties was from $42 to $47 per month while the figure for the "worst" trade specialties was from $17 to $27 per month. The cost saving from increasing the utilization rate of vocational schools was over $70 per pupil in the three-year period from 1969 to 1971.[18] And the whole of the vocational program might have been made considerably more effective if its managers had considered that helping the boys find jobs was one of their important objectives.

These partial indicators of potential X-efficiency gains should be viewed with caution since the impact of the possible changes on factors other than academic performance might be considerable. The potential cost savings shown above cannot all be added, since there are some overlaps between the different estimates of savings (for example, between points 4, 5, and 6 above). Still, the magnitudes of potential X-efficiency gains are quite large in comparison with $1.8 million gained from allocative efficiency changes. It should

175

also be recalled that these are not all of the possible X-efficiency gains and that they relate only to the lower and upper secondary levels, which account for less than 20 percent of the total education budget. If similar possibilities for cost savings were found with rsepect to primary or university education, the efficiency gains would be very much larger.

A final point with regard to comparison between X-efficiency and allocative efficiency: the X-efficiency gains considered above have been associated only with cost savings. (The possible changes are those that would not affect the output measure of academic achievement, based on Beebout's production function analysis.) Virtually nothing is known about ways in which effectiveness (measured in terms of income and employment) could be affected directly by changes in the education provided, improvements in "linkage institutions" between the schools and the labor market, or educational innovations designed to affect economic payoffs directly. These questions have not even been asked.

NOTES

1. H. Leibenstein, "Allocative Efficiency vs. 'X-Efficiency'," American Economic Review 56 (1966): 392-415.

2. W. S. Comanor and H. Leibenstein, "Allocative Efficiency, X-Efficiency and the Measurement of Welfare Losses," Economica, August 1966, pp. 304-09; A. C. Harberger, "Monopoly and Resource Allocation," American Economic Review 44 (1954): 77-87.

3. Leibenstein, op. cit., p. 395.

4. O. D. Hoerr, "Education, Income, and Equity in Malaysia," Economic Development and Cultural Change 21, no. 2 (January 1973): 260 and 272.

5. See Harberger, op. cit., pp. 81-82, and his use of an earlier formula for welfare gain from Hotelling.

6. Op. cit., p. 260.

7. A. Smith and N. L. Bennet, "Rates of Return on Investment in Education," World Year Book of Education (London: 1967); cited in M. F. Leite, et al., The Economics of Educational Costing (Lisbon: Gulbenkian Institute, 1969) 3a: 93.

8. H. Beebout, "The Production Surface for Academic Achievement: An Economic Study of Malaysian Secondary Schools," Ph.D. dissertation, University of Wisconsin at Madison, 1972).

9. Ibid., p. 200. A search for interaction effects between class size and other variables revealed no significant interactions.

10. On the other hand, see M. Blaug, An Introduction to the Economics of Education (London: Allen Lane, 1970), p. 278, for a

discussion of "the folk-lore of the small class" and questions regarding the widely held assumption that decreasing class size improves educational quality.

11. Beebout, op. cit., pp. 198-99.

12. Ibid., pp. 208-14.

13. Ibid., p. 214.

14. Ibid., p. 211. The standard deviation was 456 pupils; the range was from 250 to 2,991.

15. Department of the Treasury, Expenditure Budget, (1971), p. 421.

16. Beebout, op. cit., p. 208.

17. Ibid., pp. 203-08.

18. Expenditure Budget, op. cit., p. 421.

BIBLIOGRAPHY

BOOKS

An Asian Model of Educational Development. Paris: UNESCO, 1966.

Becker, Gary. Human Capital. New York: Columbia University Press, 1964.

Beeby, C. E. Planning and the Educational Administrator. Paris: UNESCO, 1967.

Black, Guy. Application of Systems Analysis to Government Decisions. New York: Praeger Publishers, 1969..

Blalock, Hubert M. An Introduction to Social Research. Englewood Cliffs, N. J.: Prentice-Hall, 1970.

Blaug, Mark., ed. Economics of Education: 1. Middlesex, England: Penguin Books, 1968.

_____., ed. Economics of Education: 2. Middlesex, England: Penguin Books, 1969.

_____. An Introduction to the Economies of Education. London: Allen Lane The Penguin Press, 1970.

Braybrooke, David A., and Charles E. Lindblom, A Strategy for Decision. New York: Free Press, 1963.

Buchannan, J. M., and G. Tullock, The Calculus of Consent. Ann Arbor: University of Michigan Press, 1962.

Budgeting, Programme Analysis and Cost-Effectiveness Analysis in Educational Planning. Paris: OECD, 1968.

Chase, S. B., ed. Problems in Public Expenditure Analysis. Washington, D.C.: Brookings Institution, 1965.

Chenery, Hollis., ed. Studies in Development Planning. Cambridge, Mass.: Harvard University Press, 1971.

Chesswas, J. D. Methodologies for Educational Planning for Developing Countries. Paris: UNESCO/IIEP, 1969.

Coombs, Philip H., and Jacques Hallak. Managing Educational Costs. New York: Oxford University Press, 1972.

Dechert, C. R., ed. The Social Impact of Cybernetics. Notre Dame: University of Notre Dame Press, 1966.

Dunn, E. S. Economic and Social Development: A Process of Social Learning. Baltimore: Johns Hopkins Press, 1971.

Dorfman, R. The Price System. Englewood Cliffs, N. J.: Prentice-Hall, 1964.

Do Teachers Make A Difference? U.S. Department of Health, Education and Welfare, Office of Education. Washington, D.C.: Government Printing Office, 1970.

Goldman, T. A., ed. Cost-Effectiveness Analysis. New York: Praeger Publishers, 1967.

Hansen, W. Lee., ed. Education and Income. Conference on Research on Income and Wealth. Princeton: Princeton University Press, 1970.

Hartley, Harry J. Education Planning, Programming, Budgeting: A Systems Approach. Englewood Cliffs, N. J.: Prentice-Hall, 1968.

Haveman, Robert H., and J. Margolis, eds. Public Expenditure and Policy Analysis. Chicago: Markham Publishing Company, 1971.

Hayden, H., ed. Higher Education and Development in Southeast Asia. (Vol. II) Paris: UNESCO/I.A.U., 1967.

Hinrichs, Harley and Graeme Taylor. Program Budgeting and Benefit-Cost Analysis. Pacific Palisades, California: Goodyear Publishing Company, 1969.

Hitch, Charles J. The Uses of Economics. Santa Monica, Cal.: RAND Corporation, 1960.

179

_____., and Roland N. McKean. The Economics of Defense in the Nuclear Age. Cambridge, Mass.: Harvard University Press, 1960.

Lee, Eddy. Educational Planning in West Malaysia. Kuala Lumpur, West Malaysia: Oxford University Press, 1972.

Leite, M. F. The Economics of Educational Costing. Lisbon: Gulbenkian Institute, 1969.

Lindblom, Charles E. The Policy-Making Process. Englewood Cliffs, N. J.: Prentice-Hall, 1968.

McKean, Roland N. Efficiency in Government Through Systems Analysis. New York: John Wiley & Sons, 1958.

Manpower Aspects of Educational Planning. Paris: UNESCO/IIEP, 1968.

Marglin, Stephen. Public Investment Criteria. Amsterdam: North Holland Publishing Company, 1968.

Novick, David., ed. Program Budgeting: Program Analysis and The Federal Budget. Washington, D.C.: Government Printing Office, 1964.

Papanek, Gustav F. Development Policy: Theory and Practice. Cambridge, Mass.: Harvard University Press, 1968.

Parnes, Herbert S., ed. Planning Education for Economic and Social Development. Paris: OECD, 1964.

Raiffa, Howard. Decision Analysis. Reading, Mass.: Addison-Wesley Publishing Company, 1958.

Rivlin, Alice M. Systematic Thinking for Social Action. Washington, D.C.: Brookings Institution, 1971.

Smithies, Arthur. The Budgetary Process in the United States. New York: McGraw-Hill, 1955.

Stone, Richard. Mathematics in the Social Sciences and Other Essays. London: Chapman and Hall, 1966.

Thias, H. H., and M. Carnoy. Cost-Benefit Analysis in Education: A Case Study in Kenya. Baltimore: Johns Hopkins Press, 1972.

Waterston, Albert. Development Planning—Lessons from Experience. Baltimore; Johns Hopkins Press, 1965.

Weisbrod, Burton A. External Benefits of Public Education: An Economic Analysis. Princeton: Princeton University Press, 1964.

Whitehead, Clay T. Uses and Limitations of Systems Analysis. Santa Monica: RAND Corporation (Report No. P-3683), 1967.

Wiener, Norbert. The Human Use of Human Beings. Rev. ed. New York: Doubleday & Company, 1954.

Wildavsky, Aaron. The Politics of the Budgetary Process. Boston: Little, Brown, 1964.

Williams, Walter. Social Policy Research and Analysis. New York: American Elsevier Publishing Company, 1971.

Zymelman, Manuél. Financing and Efficiency in Education. U.S. Agency for International Development, 1973.

ARTICLES

Airasian, Peter W., and George F. Madaus. "Criterion-Referenced Testing in The Classroom." Measurement in Education 3, no. 4 (May, 1972): 1-8.

Anderson, C. Arnold, and Mary Jean Bowman. "Theoretical Considerations in Educational Planning." In D. Adams, ed. Educational Planning. Syracuse: Syracuse University Press, 1964, pp. 4-46.

Arrow, Kenneth, and William M. Capron. "Dynamic Shortages and Price Rises: The Engineer-Scientist Case." Quarterly Journal of Economics 72, no. 2 (1959): 292-308.

Blaug, Mark. "The Rate of Return on Investment in Education in Great Britain." The Manchester School 33, no. 3 (1965): 205-51.

_____. "Cost-Benefit and Cost-Effectiveness Analysis in Educational Planning." In Budgeting, Programme Analysis and Cost-Effectiveness in Educational Planning. Paris: OECD, pp. 173-84.

Bowles, Samuel. "Efficient Allocation of Investment in Education." In H. Chenery, ed. Studies in Development Planning. Cambridge, Mass.: Harvard University Press, 1971, pp. 247-69.

_____. "Towards An Educational Production Function." In W. Lee Hansen, ed. Education and Income. Princeton: Princeton University Press, 1970, pp. 55-78.

Bowman, Mary Jean. "Economics of Education." Review of Educational Research 39, no. 5: pp. 641-70.

Brandl, J. E. "Education Program Analysis at HEW." In R. H. Haveman, and J. Margolis, eds. Public Expenditure and Policy Analysis. Chicago: Markham Publishing Company, 1971, pp. 461-81.

Comanor, W. S., and H. Leibenstein. "Allocative Efficiency, X-Efficiency and The Measurement of Welfare Losses." Economica (August, 1966): 304-09.

Doeringer, Peter B., and Michael. Piore. "Labor Market Adjustment and Internal Training." Industrial Relations Research Association, Proceedings of the Eighteenth Annual Meeting, pp. 1-14.

Dougherty, C. R. S. "Optimal Allocation of Investment in Education." In H. Chenery, Studies in Development Planning. Cambridge, Mass.: Harvard University Press, 1971, pp. 270-92.

Dror, Yehezkel. "The Planning Process." International Review of Administrative Sciences 29, no. 1 (Brussels: 1963): 50-52.

Dyer, H. S.; R. L. Linn; and M. J. Patton. "Feasibility Study of Educational Performance Indicators." Princeton: Educational Testing Service Staff Papers, 1967.

Eide, Kjell. "Organization of Education Planning." In D. Adams., ed. Educational Planning. Syracuse: Syracuse University Press, 1964, pp. 67-81.

Esman, M. J., and J. D. Montgomery. "Systems Approaches to Technical Cooperation: The Role of Development Administration." Public Administration Review 24 no. 5 (Sept./Oct., 1969): 507-39.

Hagen, Everett E. "Some Cultural and Personality Factors in Economic Development." Development Digest 3, no. 2 (July, 1965): 46-59.

Harberger, Arnold C. "Monopoly and Resource Allocation." American Economic Review 44 (1954): 77-87.

Harbison, Frederick. "Building A System for Assistance Activities." In E. N. Shiver, ed. Higher Education and Public International Service. Washington, D.C.: American Council on Education, 1967, pp. 44-57.

Haveman, Robert H. "Public Expenditures and Policy Analysis." In R. H. Haveman, and J. Margolis, eds. Public Expenditure and Policy Analysis. Chicago: Markham Publishing Company, 1971.

Hirschman, Albert O., and Charles E. Lindblom. "Economic Development, Research and Development, Policy Making: Some Converging Views." Behavioral Science 7 (1962): 211-22.

Hoerr, O. D. "Education, Income and Equity in Malaysia." Economic Development and Cultural Change 21, no. 2 (Jan., 1973): 247-73.

Hollister, R. G. "A Technical Evaluation of OECD's Mediterranean Regional Project and Conclusions." The World Year Book of Education. J. A. Lauwerys; Bereday; and M. Blaug, eds. Evans Brothers, 1967, pp. 161-70.

Leibenstein, Harvey. "Allocative Efficiency vs. 'X-Efficiency.'" American Economic Review 54 (1966): 392-415.

Levin, Henry M. "A Cost-Effectiveness Analysis of Teacher Selection." Journal of Human Resources 5, no. 1 (Winter, 1970): 24-33.

_____. "A New Model of School Effectiveness." In U.S. Department of Health, Education and Welfare, Office of Education, Do Teachers Make a Difference? Washington, D.C.: Government Printing Office, 1970, pp. 55-78.

Lindblom, C. E. "The Science of Muddling Through." Public Administration Review, 19 (1959): 79-88.

Lipsey, R. G., and K. Lancaster. "The General Theory of Second Best." Review of Economic Studies 24 (1956-57): 11-32.

Moser, C. A., and P. Redfern. "Education and Manpower: Some Current Research." In Models for Decision. London: The English University Press, 1964.

Parnes, Herbert S. "Manpower Analysis in Educational Planning." In H. S. Parnes, ed. Planning Education for Economic and Social Development. Paris: OECD, 1964.

_____. "Relation of Occupation to Educational Qualifications." In H. S. Parnes, ed. Planning Education for Economic and Social Development. Paris: OECD, 1964.

Phillips, H. M. "Education and Development." Investment in Education. Bangkok: UNESCO Regional Office for Education in Asia, 1967, pp. 255-98.

Prest, A. R., and R. Turvey. "Cost-Benefit Analysis: A Survey." Economic Journal (December, 1965): 683-735.

Rivlin, Alice M. "The Planning, Programming and Budgeting System in the Department of Health, Education and Welfare: Some Lessons from Experience." In R. H. Haveman, and J. Margolis, eds. Public Expenditure and Policy Analysis. Chicago: Markham Publishing Company, 1971, pp. 502-17.

Schwartz, Brita. "Introduction to Program Budgeting and Cost-Effectiveness Analysis in Educational Planning." In Budgeting, Programme Analysis and Cost Effectiveness Analysis in Educational Planning. Paris: OECD, 1968, pp. 34-47.

Smithies, Arthur. "Conceptual Framework for the Program Budget." In D. Novick, ed. Program Budgeting: Program Analysis and the Federal Budget. Washington, D.C.: Government Printing Office, 1964, pp. 2-32.

Turksen, I. B., and A. G. Holzman. "Information Design for Educational Management." Socio-Economic Planning Sciences 6 (Feb., 1972): pp. 1-20.

Wildavsky, Aaron. "Rescuing Policy Analysis from PPBS." R. H. Haveman, and J. Margolis, eds. Public Expenditure and Policy Analysis. Chicago: Markham Publishing Company, 1971, pp. 549-61.

REPORTS AND OFFICIAL PUBLICATIONS

Education in Malaysia. Kuala Lumpur, Malaysia: Dewan Bahasa dan Pustaka, 1967.

Educational Statistics of Malaysia. Kuala Lumpur: Dewan Bahasa dan Pustaka, 1970.

The Expenditure Budget of the Federal Government, 1971. Kuala Lumpur: Department of the Treasury, 1971.

Education Planning and Research Division. Jawatankuasa Di Atas Kajian Sendapat Mengenai Pelajaran Dan Masyarakat [Study of Opinion about Education and Society], Kuala Lumpur: Ministry of Education, 1973.

Government of Malaysia (Economic Planning Unit). Second Malaysian Plan, 1971-75. Kuala Lumpur: Government Printer, 1971.

_____. Treasury Economic Report, 1972-73. Kuala Lumpur: Government Printer, 1972.

Manpower Survey, 1965: States of Malaya, Technical Report. Kuala Lumpur: Malaysian Department of Statistics, 1966.

Malaysian Socio-Economic Survey of Households, 1967-68. Kuala Lumpur: Malaysian Department of Statistics, 1971.

"Objectives and Procedures of the Michigan State Assessment Program—1970-71." Lansing, Michigan: Michigan Department of Education, Assessment Report No. 7, December, 1970.

Razak, Tun Abdul. Report on the Education System of Malaya. Kuala Lumpur: Federal Legislative Council Paper No. 21, 1956.

"Report of the Commission on Teachers' Salaries." Kuala Lumpur: 1971.

Report of the Education Review Committee. (Rahman Talib Report)
Kuala Lumpur: Government Printer, 1964.

Report of the Higher Education Planning Committee. Kuala Lumpur:
1967. Mimeographed.

UNPUBLISHED MATERIAL

Beebout, Harold S. "EPRD Secondary School Survey: Preliminary
Report," Kuala Lumpur, Malaysia: Ministry of Education,
Education Planning and Research Division, 1971. Mimeographed.

_____. "The Production Surface for Academic Achievement: An
Economic Study of Malaysian Secondary Education." Ph.D.
dissertation, University of Wisconsin at Madison, 1972.

Dyer, Henry S. "The Concept and Utility of Educational Performance
Indicators." Paper read at the Systems and Cybernetics Conference, Boston, Mass., October, 1967. Mimeographed.

Hoerr, O. D. "Economic Growth Requirements for Education."
Memorandum to Thong Yaw Hong, Director, Economic Planning
Unit, Prime Minister's Department. Kuala Lumpur, Malaysia:
1969. Mimeographed.

Kleindorfer, G. B., and L. M. S. Roy. "A Model for Educational
Planning in East Pakistan," Dacca: Pakistan-Berkeley Program
in Educational Planning, Ford Foundation, 1969. Mimeographed.

_____.; M. D. White; and C. S. Benson. "A Planning and Imple-
mentation Model for Vocational Education," Dacca: Pakistan-
Berkeley Program in Educational Planning, Ford Foundation,
1970. Mimeographed.

Lourdesamy, I. "The Vocational School Program in Malaysia: A
Study in Effective Development Administration." Ph.D. dissertation, University of Pittsburgh, 1972.

Manheim, M. L., and F. L. Hall. Abstract Representation of Goals:
A Method for Making Decisions in Complex Problems. Cambridge, Mass.: Massachusetts Institute of Technology, Department of Civil Engineering, 1965.

McMeekin, Robert W. "Analysis of Educational Expenditure Decision in Developing Countries." Ph.D. dissertation, Harvard University, 1973.

_____. "Systems Planning—The Uses and Limitations of a Systems Approach to Education Planning," Kuala Lumpur: Ministry of Education, Education Planning and Research Division Staff Paper, 1971. Mimeographed.

Sheath, R. H., and D. J. Vickery. "Secondary General School Buildings in Malaysia—Their Functions, Utilization and Costs." Colombo, Ceylon: Asian Regional Institute for School Building Research. A preliminary report, 1971. Mimeographed.

"SRM/Ford Social and Economic Survey, West Malaysia/1968." Special tabulation of market research data performed for The Ford Foundation, Kuala Lumpur, by Survey Research Malaysia, 1970. Mimeographed.

Tobias, George. "Education Planning in Economic Development: A Proposal for Malaysia," Kuala Lumpur: The Ford Foundation, Report of Program Advisor to the Minister of Education, 1968.

BIBLIOGRAPHIES

Systems Analysis for Educational Planning: A Selected, Annotated Bibliography. Paris: OECD, 1969.

sis, 27; use in program budgeting, 28
cost-utility analysis, 26
costs (see educational expenditure
analysis)
cybernetics, 3-4, 6, 35, 42, 134

data (information), aggregated and
disaggregated, 55-56, 62; for
use in economic analysis, 104-
106, 137-138; for use in educational planning, 2-5, 7, 18-19,
21-22, 29-30, 35-36; for use in
manpower analysis, 10-14; for
use in rate-of-return analysis,
17-18, 43; on performance, 57,
63-64, 129; policy use in Malaysian case study, 95-103, 123-125,
153-157 (see also research,
macronegative and micropositive
information)
data gathering, for decision-making,
making, 137-138; for manpower
analysis, 10-14, 33; for rate-of-
return analysis, 16-18; in Malaysian secondary school survey,
153-158; policy-relevant data,
56-57, 63-64, 129 [cost effectiveness of, 64-65, 138; criteria,
58-61; operational characteristics, 61-65; types of surveys
needed, 59, 63-65, 87]; problems
in, 20-21, 40-44, 46, 54-58
Dechert, C. R., 21
"decision theory," 48-49
decisions and decision-making, 6,
29, 31-36, 39-40, 42; characteristics of, 47-50; hierarchy of
decisions, 30-31
Dorfman, R., 51
Dougherty, C. R. S., 16, 23, 86
dropout rates (see wastage rates)
Dror, Yehezkel, 5-6
Dunn, E. S., 23
Dyer, Henry S., 53, 69, 155

EPRD (see Education Planning and
Research Division, Ministry of
Education, Malaysia)
ETS (see Educational Testing Service, Princeton, N.J.)
earnings (see wages)
economic analysis and choices,
compared to "needs oriented"
planning, 43-44; limits of use-
fullness, 46-50; use in educational planning, 1-3, 4-5, 20-26,
28-29, 32, 35, 39, 43-44, 46-47,
103-106 (see also educational
expenditure analysis, rate-of-
return analysis)
education, effect on socioeconomic
change, 15-17, 133, 134; resistance to change in, 44-45
education of planners, 139-140
Education Planning and Research
Division (EPRD), Ministry of
Education, Malaysia, 74, 98n,
111, 122, 139, 147, 153, 155,
157-158
education plans (documents), 32,
33-36, 45 (see also First Malaysia Plan, Second Malaysia Plan)
education system of Malaysia (see
Malaysia, education system)
educational alternatives (see alternatives in education)
educational expenditure analysis,
3-4, 19, 21, 29-30, 39-40, 50,
94, 104; analysis procedure, 28-
29, 40-46; cost implications of
alternative admission policies,
79-80; hierarchy of decisions
in, 29-31; importance of altered
orientation in, 130-133; relative
costs of Malayasian science and
arts education, 96-97; relative
costs of Malayasian technical
education, 99; relative costs of
Malayasian vocational education,
121-123; secondary school sur-

McKean, Roland N., 25, 31, 51, 52, 126n
McMeekin, Robert W., 52, 53, 166
"macronegative" information, 56
Madaus, G. F., 53
Malay language instruction medium, 88-92, 142-143, 145; National University, 147; science stream, 95-96, 97-98
Malay—non-Malay population, employment ratios, 90-91; enrollment ratios, 88-89
Malaysia, case study of upper secondary educational policy, 70-106; [criticisms of case study, 126-127; data used in, 74-75; objectives, 70-71; policy alternatives for growth rate, 71-73, 77]; education system, 142-151; [budget, 150-151; goals, 142, 144; history, 142-144; structure, 144-147]; First Malaysia Plan, 83, 110-111, 124-125, 150; Second Malaysia Plan, 88, 95, 111, 124; vocational education, 110-125 (see also longitudinal survey of vocational school graduates in Malaysia, manpower study in Malaysia, secondary general school buildings in Malaysia, secondary school survey of Malaysia, socioeconomic survey of West Malaysia)
Malaysian Certificate of Education (MCE) (see MCE Examination)
Malaysian Certificate of Vocational Education (MCVE) (see MCVE Examination)
Malaysian Examination Syndicate, 149
Manheim, M. L., 53
manpower analysis and planning, critique of, 9-14, 33, 38-39, 44n,

104-105, 123, 130; uses of, 13-14, 33, 104-105, 109
manpower study in Malaysia, 74, 80-84, 90, 105, 111, 124, 150; conflict with Malaysian rate-of-return analysis, 84-85; occupational profile of labor force, 82
Marglin, Stephen, 51, 52
Margolis, J., 51, 52
Mediterranean Regional Project, 130
Michigan, Department of Education, 42
"micropositive" information, 56, 66, 129
Ministry of Education, Malaysia. Education Planning and Research Division (see Education Planning and Research Division (EPRD), Ministry of Education, Malaysia)
Ministry of Education, Malaysia. Technical Division (see Technical Division, Ministry of Education, Malaysia)
models, use of, 9, 26, 31, 65; flow model of enrollment, 65, 160-166
Montgomery, J. D., 141
Moser, C. A., 23

national needs and goals, 8, 88
National University, Malaysia, 147
"needs approach" to planning, 9, 44-45
Novick, David, 51

OECD, 23, 51
objectives (see goals)
on-job training, 10, 105
optimality and optimization, 6, 8, 30, 32, 40-41, 47, 50
Overseas School Certificate, 148

PPBS (see program budgeting)
Papanek, Gustav F., 21
Parnes, Herbert S., 23

Patton, M. J., 155
Penang Free School, 143
Phillips, H. M., 22
planning, educational (see educational planning)
plans, education (documents) (see education plans [documents])
policy analysis and research (see data [information])
political considerations in planning, 6-7, 8-9, 29, 45, 49, 72, 77, 87-88, 89-90 (see also equity and educational opportunity)
Polytechnic Institute, Malaysia, 145
Prest, A. R., 21, 52
private rate of return, 14n, 85, 85n
production function analysis, 20, 39, 43, 43n, 153, 154, 176; "The Production Surface for Academic Achievement," 75, 153-158
program budgeting, 21, 27-29; compared to systems analysis, 28; expenditure data in, 58-59; in education sector, 28, 151
programming, planning and budgeting systems (PPBS) (see program budgeting)
"promotion pass" rate, 72, 89
public expenditure analysis, 25-29 (see also educational expenditure analysis)
public expenditure decisions, hierarchy of choices, 31

quantifiability of information, 48, 50 (see also data gathering)
quantitative projections, 7-9; of enrollment, 75-77

Rahman Talib, Abdul, 144
rate-of-return analysis, and x-efficiency, 167-176; based on socio-economic survey of West

Malaysia, 74, 84, 85, 100-103; conflict with Malaysian Manpower study, 84-85; strengths and weaknesses, 14-18, 19-20, 33, 38-39, 42-43, 86-87; use of data on unemployment in, 85-87
Razak, Tun Abdul, 143
Redfern, P., 23
"remove" year, 143
research, priorities, 68; relationship to planning, 137-138; suggested projects, 65-69 (see also data gathering)
resource allocation (see allocation of resources)
resource-effectiveness analysis, 26
Rivlin, Alice, 63, 141
rural trade schools, 111, 149-150

SMP (see Second Malaysia plan)
SRP (Examination), 71, 89, 91
sample surveys, suggested topics, 66-69; value of, 64-65
Schwartz, Brita, 53
science education, 95-98, 145; need for increase in, 96; rate of return compared to arts and technical graduates, 100-103; relative costs of science and arts education, 96-97
Second Malaysia plan, 88, 95, 111, 124
secondary education in Malaysia (see Malaysia)
Secondary School Survey of Malaysia, 75, 90-94, 106-107; description of survey and methodology, 153-158; variables [used in linear model of student achievement, 156; other variables gathered, 155]
Sekolah Lanjutang Kampong, 111, 149-150
Sheath, R. H., 107

193

wastage rates, 89, 147-148
Waterston, Albert, 19, 24, 35
Weisbrod, Burton A., 23
West Malaysia (see Malaysia)
Whitehead, Clay T., 49, 51, 52, 53,
Wiener, Norbert, 4, 54
Wildavsky, Aaron, 28, 52
Williams, Walter, 56
Wilson, Alan B., 147
women, enrollment ratios, 90, 147
World Bank, 20; analysis of

Malaysian manpower needs, 81-83,
111, 124-125, 150

"x-efficiency", 37-39, 128, 131;
compared to allocative efficiency,
175-176; in Malaysian case study,
105-106, 123-124; savings in
Malaysian education system,
129-138 (see also efficiency
and inefficiency in education)

ROBERT W. McMEEKIN, Jr., is an economist who has served as consultant to the governments of El Salvador, Nicaragua, Malaysia, and Canada, as well as domestic agencies of the U.S. government. He has been employed by the Ford Foundation, the U.S. Agency for International Development, and several private consulting firms. His work has concerned economic and regional development with particular emphasis upon planning for social sector development, especially the education sector.

Dr. McMeekin holds a Bachelors degree from Yale University, a Masters in International Relations from the University of Kentucky and a Masters in Public Administration from the Kennedy School of Government, Harvard University. His Ph.D. is the Joint Degree in Political Economy and Government, also from Harvard.

RELATED TITLES
Published by
Praeger Special Studies

EDUCATION AND DEVELOPMENT RECONSIDERED:
The Bellagio Conference Papers
Ford Foundation/Rockefeller Foundation
edited by F. Champion Ward

EDUCATION, MANPOWER, AND DEVELOPMENT IN
SOUTH AND SOUTHEAST ASIA
M. Shamsul Huq

EDUCATIONAL PROBLEMS OF DEVELOPING
SOCIETIES: With Case Studies of Ghana and Pakistan
Adam Curle

NON-FORMAL EDUCATION: An Annotated Bibliography
edited by Rolland G. Paulston